The Glastonbury Festivals

BY

LYNNE ELSTOB AND ANNE HOWES

Design: Roy Avis and Alan Peacock

Typesetters: PCS Typesetting, Frome, Somerset.

thanks to Colin, Chris, Roy, Alan, Mid-Somerset CND, Mike and Jean Eavis, Jamie, Rupert, Robert, John Andrews, Fay Weldon, Barren Down Surgery, Andrew Kerr, Pat Thompson and Henri Otani, Charlie Wrighton, Penny Mellor, David Burton, Alan Blandford, Mike Orchard, Meg Beresford, Arabella Churchill, Stephanie Leland, Carey, Mark and Helen Cann, John Wheat, Nick Scholefield, Maxine and Terry Horrocks, Josie Hiscox, Dan Plesch, Pat Wilson, David Ansonia, Charlie and Paul, Tony Hollingsworth, Jo and Ian Dennis, Mid-Somerset Series of Newspapers, Keith Furlonger and Mr. Elson.

and the photographers: Tim Malyon, Jan Hammond, Neil Cooper, Bob Cannings, Tony Emery, Cathy Appleton, Erica Smith, Marcus Cole, Donald Scaife, Jeremy Hooper, Andy Liguz, Brian Walker, Ron Reid, Kevin Redpath, Paul Walters.

Publishers: GOTHIC IMAGE PUBLICATIONS *and* CAHLME

ISBN 0-906362-10-5

CONTENTS

to our children
Catherine, Daniel, Christopher and Robert

"If there is to be peace
in this world, some hope
lies in the younger generations
and these festivals are for them
just as much as for us
older festival goers"

Michael and Jean Eavis.

FOREWORD

Seventeen years ago the original Worthy Farm Festival happened here, and from that moment on the place has never been quite the same. Every year the thing gets bigger and more and more of our lives gets drawn into this huge machine of phones, bills, meetings, negotiations, post mortems, and plans and ideas for the future.

I suppose I started it all partly from boredom with years and years of just milking, but the influence of those late '60s festivals started me off. I thought there might be a way of combining the traditional country fairs with the ideals of the pop festival culture, where people could come together and have a good time in a more relaxed way than those huge stadium gigs! By adding theatre, drama, alternative politics and kids' entertainments it would broaden the scope of appeal and could become part of a regular midsummer festival of joy and celebration of life.

Volumes could be written about the festival, but hopefully this book will give you an insight into some of the brighter and happier moments that have happened in these fields of ours.

Michael Eavis

***I am going a long way . . .
To the island-valley of Avilion;
Where falls not hail, or rain, or any snow,
Nor ever wind blows loudly; but it lies
Deep-meadow'd, happy, fair with orchard lawns
And bowery hollows crown'd with summer sea . . .***

from Tennyson's "Morte d'Arthur"

INTRODUCTION

As the sun disappears behind the ruins of St. Michael's Church on the mystical summit of Glastonbury Tor, the gently sloping pastures of the lush green Vale of Avalon take on more muted tones, and the last remaining rays of light fall on a strange metallic structure — the Glastonbury Pyramid.

Erected as a farm building in 1981, it has since become for thousands of people the focal point of the Festivals which are now the largest fund-raising events for the Campaign for Nuclear Disarmament.

However, the story of the Festivals at Worthy Farm really begins eleven years earlier, in the aftermath of Flower Power, pyschedelia and the swinging sixties . . .

1970 19th to 20th September

THE FIRST FESTIVAL

Worthy Farm stands on the edge of the pretty Somerset village of Pilton. From there you look across five miles of flat fields to the sudden hummocky hill of Glastonbury, which dominates the surrounding countryside. Nowhere could the Tor be better seen than from Worthy Farm, whose lands circle and enclose the western slopes of Pilton. The Eavis family, hard-working dairy farmers, staunch Methodists, had lived there for generations playing their part in village life. The farm had little to distinguish it from a dozen others in the area; that is until 1970, when things began to change.

Flower power, long hair, social revolution, the excitement of change, the sheer noise and charge of rock music, reached this small Somerset village. Nothing has been the same there since.

What happened was that in June 1970 the unsuspecting Michael Eavis went along to the Blues Festival at the Bath and West Showground. What a concert that was! 200,000 delighted fans rocked on for 48 hours to the music of Led Zeppelin, Pink Floyd, Steppenwolf, The Byrds, Santana — and who cared that the organisation was shambolic, Somerset had known nothing like it.

An inspired Michael returned to Worthy with the beginnings of an idea for a festival of his own, though on a much smaller scale. A September date was fixed and word got round. With the last of the hay gathering completed all was ready for the 2,500 who turned up. There was free milk, music from Marc Bolan and T. Rex, peace, love, friendship, but little commercialism. Many of those who knew Michael were concerned for his sanity — this was after all a highly uncharacteristic venture for an up till then very conventional farmer. One more than satisfied fan said "Mr. Eavis deserves a knighthood for making everyone so happy". However, the village rather hoped it would all go away.

But of course it didn't. How could it?

GLASTONBURY FAYRE

News of this "hippy" festival spread widely. Among those who heard was the charismatic Andrew Kerr, who for many years had been Randolph Churchill's personal assistant and close companion. Churchill's death in 1968 left Andrew uncertain about the future, and it was then he began writing his book "Heaven is a Planet".

At this time music was once again becoming a very powerful means of spiritual expression through its links with Flower Power and mystics from the East. In 1970 Andrew went to the Bath Blues Festival and the record-breaking Isle of Wight Festival, but was shocked by their commercialism. As he wrote in 1974 "Driving back to London I became full of enthusiasm and started planning what I hoped would be a truly free festival". He did — The Glastonbury Fayre 1971.

At the time, Stonehenge seemed the ideal site, but financial backing was unavailable and the looming presence of the Ministry of Defence, who control most of Salisbury Plain, led Andrew to consider Glastonbury.

Knowing that a festival had just been held at Worthy Farm his hopes were high when he telephoned Michael Eavis to arrange a meeting. After an all-night vigil on the Tor, he visited Worthy Farm and met Michael for the first time. All doubt was swept away. Towards the end of 1970 Andrew moved into the farmhouse. With Arabella Churchill and other friends he formed Solstice Capers Limited and together they planned the 1971 Glastonbury Fayre. This was to be a free festival "in the mediaeval tradition with music, dance, poetry, theatre, lights and the opportunity for spontaneous entertainment".

Before long, flowing robes and Indian beads began to appear amongst the overalls and Wellington boots, and the pungent aroma of burning incense mingled with the familiar farmyard smells. Those involved reminisce about this time with emotion, although their memories of all the long discussions into the night both about the Fayre and every other conceivable topic are somewhat blurred sixteen years on.

As the summer solstice approached, news of the planned festival spread and many people appeared at the farm to help with preparations. Although some of these unpaid workers were willing and energetic, others were content to laze about the farm. Inevitably, the original small group of organisers shouldered most of the work and they tried hard to provide facilities, co-operating closely with the local authorities, but lack of organisational skills, an inadequate labour force and the non-arrival of promised materials such as wood meant that only very basic amenities materialised.

It was decided that only vegetarian food should be available and that no alcohol should be sold on site. Headrest of Yeovil produced lentil soup at 4p a bowl; Bath Arts Workshop, curried beans and rice at 5p a portion; Communal Knead supplied free bread and vegetable stew; the Digger Action Movement gave away free boiled eggs, muesli, porridge, lentil soup and stew, and Civil Aid provided hot coffee and soup at night as well as meals for stage crew and technicians. Civil Aid reckoned it was possible to make 10 gallons of lentil soup for £1.64 from Headrest's recipe of 14 lb. lentils, 6 lb. onions, and 6 lb. potatoes!

First Aid was available in the farmhouse, courtesy of the British Red Cross Society with a team of doctors led by local G.P. Alan Blandford working a shift system throughout the Fayre. Other welfare services on hand included a Jesus Tent, Release, Samaritans, Civil Aid and the Environmental Health Department who made sure water supplies were maintained, food kept reasonably hygenic and toilets as clean as possible. The loos were constructed out of scaffolding poles draped with hessian screens, perched above a trench. Some were positioned under the high power electricity cables which cross the site so the Glastonbury vibes were indeed felt at every visit! Other services included information, water, telephones and a marquee site for traders.

The first pilgrims arrive

The first Pyramid Stage was constructed by Bill Harkin and his crew out of scaffolding and expanded metal covered with plastic sheeting. The structure was built close to the Glastonbury Abbey/Stonehenge ley line and over the site of a blind spring. This precise location was chosen as it was believed that at such a place ancient earth forces could be harnessed and the earth revitalized during the Fayre. This too was the perfect site for a stage, positioned as it was in a natural amphitheatre.

The pyramid shape is said to be a very powerful structure, the apex of which draws energy up and transmits it still further whilst the energy from the stars and the sun is attracted to it and drawn down. Those who saw the original Glastonbury Pyramid at night liken it to a diamond as huge arc lights reflected off the metal sheeting. The energy was almost tangible as people danced on the stage alongside the bands.

Andrew Kerr: "Musicians are coming to play, many of them because they feel the magic of Glastonbury and the Vale of Avalon, some because they 'dig' playing for you, free, and all of them because they want to.

"Glastonbury is a place far too beautiful for yet another rock festival. If the Festival has a specific intention it is to create an increase of awareness in the power of the Universe, a heightening of consciousness and a recognition of our place in the function of this our tired and molested planet.

"We have spent too long telling the Universe to shut up, we must search for the humility to listen. The earth is groaning for contact with our ears and eyes. Universal awareness touches gently at our shoulders, we are creators being created and we must prove our worth.

"These are the ideals which have inspired the Fayre."

AGW 116G

Featured on stage were the Pink Fairies, Melanie, Fairport Convention, Traffic, Brinsley Schwarz, Hawkwind, Arthur Brown, the Edgar Broughton Band, Skin Alley and the legendary David Bowie. After the festival, in 1972, these musicians recorded a now very rare triple album set which was produced by Revelation Enterprises. It included tracks donated by Pete Townshend and Marc Bolan and one whole side from the Grateful Dead whose presence had been anticipated at the Fayre, but who, for reasons which remain vague, never actually arrived.

Music was subject to a midnight curfew which was fairly loosely adhered to. However, on the first night Michael realised that things were going on far too long. Knowing the ultimate responsibility to be his, he went down to the stage to sort things out. A little later he was seen chasing Mick Brown, one of the stage crew, round and round in full view of the crowd (thanks to strong lighting and transparent plastic sheeting) and to the accompaniment of the still very loud music. Suddenly Mick was no longer there. He'd taken off his glasses, cap, jacket and wig and developed a limp! Making his reappearance, he walked straight past Michael who didn't recognise him. Nevertheless, Michael saw to it that the music was stopped, and the stacks of speakers fell silent.

Loud nocturnal music was not the only phenomenon hitherto unknown in the village. The previously inclement weather improved tremendously during the Fayre, causing many people to cast off their clothes along with their inhibitions. Quite an unusual sight in deepest rural Somerset! Instead of tents, some people slept in plastic bags or used torn-off tree branches to cover themselves at night. Although planned only to celebrate the solstice, from the first arrivals to the last departures, the whole event actually lasted several weeks. Of course all of this led to rumblings of discontent in the locality. There were no more official festivals at Worthy Farm until 1979.

The 1971 Glastonbury Fayre certainly had its problems but many of the estimated 12,000 who were there enjoyed the experience and felt it to be a turning point in their lives. They saw it as a vision of what the Age of Aquarius could achieve with less emphasis on material possessions and more on sharing and caring, shown by these two extracts from the record booklet —

There were no anxious faces, torn betting slips or broken bottles and spirits at Glastonbury . . . Last week in the low cold light of December I sat on a plank amongst the gravel where the Pyramid had stood in the early summer . . . in the lush green damp grass growing in front of the stage and beyond across the rolling green there was no visible sign that a great happening had occurred . . . All the marks of our activity had grown back into the good earth . . . But in the chill you could feel the everlasting warmth of love and see the visions of joyful dancing and hear the music of life and know that the meek will inherit the earth . . . and when man has ravaged the planet with his overpopulations . . . excessive thermal energy demands . . . gluttony . . . and we have to build again then it will be done with love and concern for our brothers and sisters and the realisation that our little planet circling beautifully in space is what God gave us to make our heaven from . . ."

A rainbow did actually appear in the sky on a hot afternoon at Glastonbury.

I saw it, honest.

We didn't have a religious experience, but in a strange way we found some kind of enlightenment.

We discovered a confirmation that if our culture is left to itself it can survive.

We are able to live in harmony with each other. Ten thousand or more people, living for nearly a week in tents and makeshift shelter, were able to keep it together through five days of hot sunshine, a torrential rain, laughing, dancing, sharing food, dope and shelter, listening to rock and roll and throughout maintaining a community that lived peaceably without the need for restriction or authority.

Sure a few people had stuff ripped off, sure some trees were cut down, and people had bummers some got lonely and others got sunburnt.

Nobody says there weren't problems.

But they got solved; maybe the solutions weren't the best, but the problems were solved and the people came together and kept it together.

The free festivals like Phun City and Glastonbury gave a glimpse of alternative ways in which people could live their lives outside the present death culture.

This album is a memorial to what was achieved in those five days; that makes it valuable.

The most valuable thing is not that the vision of five days in Glastonbury is only remembered, but that the vision is repeated and extended until it becomes reality."

Between 1972 and 1978 at the time of the summer solstice, people made pilgrimages to the place where the original Pyramid had stood. Some brought with them flowers which they laid on the rough stone foundations — the only visible indication of the vast structure that had been the Glastonbury Pyramid — and there, amidst the rubble, huge moon daisies grew.

AN IMPROMPTU FESTIVAL

One day in the middle of June, Michael Eavis happened to pass some travellers on the road near Pilton, and recognised the familiar assortment of gaily painted vans and buses, some with teepee poles lashed to their roofs. When he stopped to chat to them (and their police escort) the travellers told him they were headed for Worthy Farm and that there was going to be a festival there! Washed out from Stonehenge and evicted from Kennard Moor by irate farmers armed with muck spreaders and a bull, they had come to seek refuge at Worthy. So, after some discussion back at the farm, a free 'mini' festival took place, attended by about 500 people. They came on foot, on horseback, in gypsy caravans, in cars, and in the rain! Someone even arrived with a collapsible pyramid on a trailer.

At the time, in a caravan behind the farmhouse, there lived a man who was a socialist writer and something of a recluse. He didn't approve of festivals, and hated the assault on his privacy. However, even he made his contribution to the event, although whether or not he meant to is unclear. The stage needed power — the nearest convenient supply was in the caravan. So his cooker was disconnected, a handful of 10p pieces fed into the meter and a line run to the stage!

Although there was very little organisation and few facilities laid on for this impromptu festival, somehow it didn't matter. The good nature of the people, their self-discipline and awareness of how to adapt helped create a near perfect environment in this most beautiful of places.

THE YEAR OF THE CHILD

This Fayre was held with the purpose of "creating a beneficial vibration for all those present, and consequently for the planet as a whole". The aim was not only to provide a location at the time of the summer solstice where people could gather together to listen to music, but also to raise money for the United Nations' Year of the Child.

Bill Harkin and Arabella Churchill were the instigators on this occasion, and Michael Eavis helped to back it financially by offering the deeds of his farm to the bank in return for a substantial loan. This enabled the Fayre to go ahead as planned and tickets went on sale at £5 for 3 days, £4 for 2 days and £3 for the last day.

Work began erecting the various stages and marquees, setting up the Market Area and laying on electricity supplies around the 150 acre site. "Roundabout" lavatories were installed in various places and water was supplied in huge barrels. At each water point washing-up bowls and soap were provided!

A team of local doctors and nurses backed up by the Red Cross operated from a large marquee in the welfare area, and nearby alternative medicine was represented by a variety of healers, masseurs, homeopaths and acupuncturists. Release provided legal advice and drug counselling, while Samaritans were on hand to help with emotional problems. Civil Aid set up and operated a field telephone communications system, ran cheap mass catering facilities and cleaned the lavatories on site.

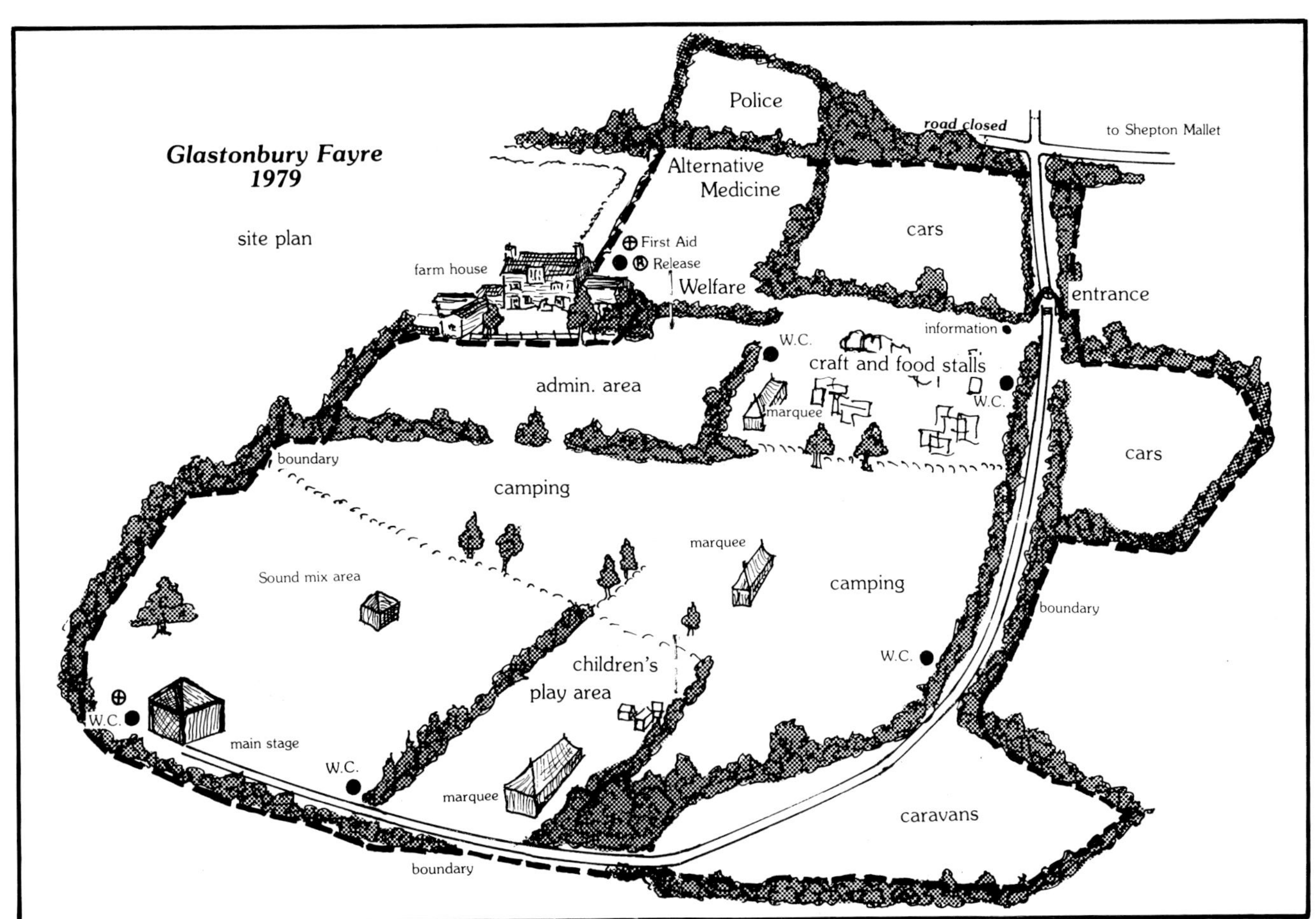

Arabella foresaw that many people at the Fayre would bring young children with them and felt strongly that special provision should be made for them. There should be a place where they could play happily and safely, enjoying their own entertainment. And so, with the help of her friend Mike Orchard, she established the Children's Area with its adventure playground, art workshops, inflatables, children's theatre, paddling pools, sandpits, clowns and puppets. From this conception in children's entertainment was born the Children's World charity, which is now well established throughout the Somerset and Avon area bringing music and drama experience through creative play to many handicapped children.

Arabella's other innovation was the Theatre Area where fringe entertainers could perform for those who hadn't come along just for the music. Francis Salter took on the organisation and engaged acts such as Incubus, Footsbarn, All Women's Cabaret, Centre Ocean Stream and the Natural Theatre Company.

On the main stage (supplied courtesy of Genesis), Peter Gabriel and Steve Hillage topped the bill. Also during the three-day event, the Alex Harvey Band and the recently formed Sky were among other bands to entertain the crowds.

There was plenty of good feeling. It was as though the sleeping children of the early festivals had awoken, coming together again in an appointed place at this very special time. On the whole those present had a great deal of respect for their environment, other people and for the Fayre itself. But, although about 12,000 people came, the organisers suffered a huge financial loss and no-one wanted to risk another festival in 1980.

Bands

INTRODUCED BY PETE DRUMMOND

Aswad Decline and Fall Ginger Baker Gong Gordon Giltrap Hawkwind John Cooper Clarke Judy Tzuke Matumbi New Order Nick Pickett Robert Hunter Roy Harper Supercharge Taj Mahal Talisman Tim Blake

(Other bands have indicated their desire to play but do not wish to be publicised)
There will also be a number of speakers including
Bruce Kent, Edward P. Thompson and Sir George Trevelyan

Theatre and films

European Theatre of War, Eye to Eye, Matchbox Purveyors, Tony Crerar, Greatest Show on Legs, Ekome, Attic, Crystal Theatre, Forkbeard Fantasy, Dance Tales, White Horse, Skullduggery, Emerging Dragon Blowsabella, Fire-eaters.
Films showing every night from 9pm – 3.30am

Children's Area

Inflatables by Airspace and Groundwell, Palfi the Clown, Zippo, Ekome (African tribal dancers), Jacolly Puppets, Bath Puppets, Donkey Team, Bristol Playbus, Steam Railway, Playskool, Plus, Adventure Playground, Stage and Marquees.

In addition to the above events there will also be a large market area, food stalls, medical and legal services and free camping. Three day advance tickets are £8 each, children up to 14 years old get in free. The fee for a stall is £40 this entitles two people to trade at the Festival for three days.

Applications for TICKETS to:– C.N.D. (Festival) 11 Goodwin Street, London N4 3HQ. Applications for STALLS to:– Festival Office, Worthy Farm, Pilton, Shepton Mallet, Somerset BA4 4BY. All Cheques and Postal Orders to be made payable to GLASTONBURY C.N.D. FESTIVAL. Please enclose an S.A.E. with your applications.

GLASTONBURY C N D FESTIVAL 1981
WORTHY FARM PILTON SOMERSET
CND
Glastonbury
19 FRI 20 SAT 21 SUN JUNE
THREE DAY TICKET
£8
No 01321

PROGRAMME

THE FIRST CND FESTIVAL

A new decade had dawned and with it came the realisation for many people that the world was playing with a very dangerous toy — the nuclear weapon. Membership of the Campaign for Nuclear Disarmament grew steadily, reflecting a slow but sure change in public opinion, reinforcing the revelation that those who believe in nuclear disarmament are not "reds under the bed" but sensible, clear-thinking, peace-loving people. Now, Worthy Farm may be deep in the Somerset countryside but it is not too remote to be touched by this rejuvenation in the Peace Movement. Early in 1981, after a well attended public meeting in a local school hall, Mid-Somerset CND was formed, bringing the issue very near to home. It soon became clear to Michael and Jean Eavis that they could help positively by holding festivals at their farm as benefits for the Campaign.

Michael arranged a meeting with the treasurer of National CND and found that he had a certain amount of convincing to do. The previous festivals had been financial disasters causing an understandable reticence. However, Michael's powers of persuasion are considerable. He was sure that with proper management instead of the previous committee style of organisation, he could make the festival into a profitable venture. Agreement was reached whereby National CND would send out information in their mailings, handle advance ticket sales, and allow the use of the CND logo, Michael being responsible for providing the necessary money, arranging the entertainment and organising the event in general.

For the first time Michael was actively involved in all arrangements, liaising with local authorities, managing the volunteer site workforce building the new pyramid stage, booking the bands, organising the market stalls, even delivering information mailings to CND's national office in the back of an old Morris pick-up. These were nearly distributed prematurely when the packaging was torn open by the wind on the M4 causing a cloud of printed sheets to float along the carriageway. As there was not too much traffic, Michael stopped the pick-up and stayed with it to secure the rest of the load while Jean rushed along the hard-shoulder collecting as much of the unintended litter as possible!

Early on in the preparations it was decided to build a new pyramid on almost the same spot as the 1971 stage. This time, however, it would be a permanent structure, doubling as a cowshed and animal foodstore during the winter months. The original pyramid had been a beautiful sight when lit up at night but rather odd in daylight and had almost collapsed at one point. The new one had to be made of stronger stuff. A great deal of thought and planning went into its construction. The wooden framework was local timber and unwanted telegraph poles but the roofing was a problem for a long time.

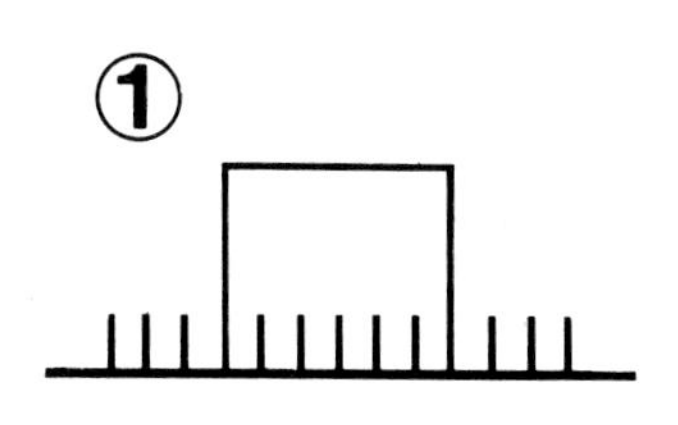

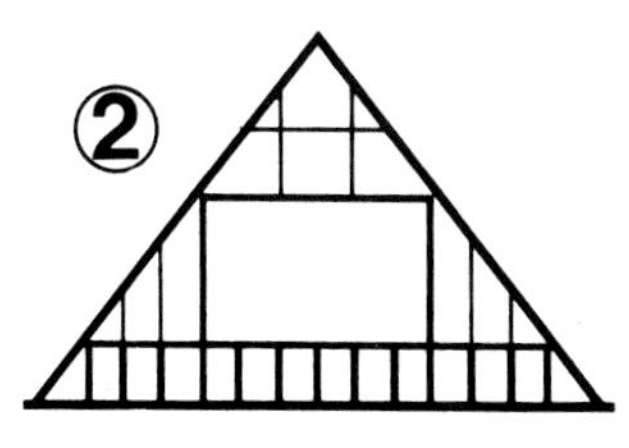

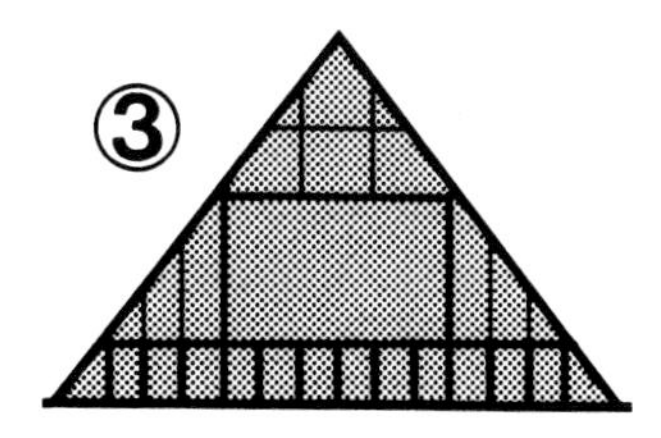

1. The telegraph poles are cut to length and embedded in the hard-core base.

2. The Douglas Firs *(Pseudotsuga Menziesii)* are bolted into position and the pyramid takes shape.

3. On goes the cladding. The last panel is hoisted into position minutes before the first band hits the stage.

Work began in appalling weather in May, foundations were dug and the wooden structure erected. But soon there were unforeseen problems. Michael had hoped the 80′ square, 50′ high pyramid would qualify as a farm building and therefore not need to comply so strictly with planning laws, but it was, in fact, just too tall. As well as a certificate to show it would meet building regulations and would not be dangerous, it also needed formal planning permission. It was a race against time to process the necessary forms and certificates. However, the festival itself was safe since no banning orders could be brought into force in time. Michael's main worry was the future of the CND festivals. "What we fear most is that Mendip (District Council) will think we have been trying to trick them and will refuse us planning permission in the future."

While all this was going on, the pyramid roof was still to be finalised. Thatch? Tiles? Corrugated iron? Michael stood firm that he wanted it silver-coloured but ordinary corrugated iron was not right. Then one day while buying cows at Taunton market he came across a certain Mr. Coates with an enormous quantity of box-section iron sheets for sale. One look was enough to reveal its potential. On learning that it was surplus to requirements at the Ministry of Defence, Michael was delighted — it would be the crowning glory — the perfect irony. He bought the lot! Back at the farm, the builders were not too sure at first but as soon as they leant a few pieces against the framework,they too were convinced. It was finished just in time except that the wooden CND logo proved too heavy to lift into its position at the apex and spent its first festival at the front corner of the stage.

By this time most of the arrangements had been made: the bands had been booked; the new Children's area organised with permanent wooden structures; the market area given its new site; a comprehensive welfare service arranged; theatre was looking good — once again Arabella Churchill took on the responsibility for this area. Towards the end though, Michael realised he needed help and began to call in trusted friends. Andrew Kerr took care of site management, Tony Hollingsworth sorted out the mess in the office and made breakfast for the crew, Mark Cann of Mid-Somerset CND was called in three days before the event to run an information service.

Miraculously, everything came together in time to welcome about 18,000 people, many of whom had travelled hundreds of miles to be there. To keep a check on numbers and to make sure that everyone paid their £8 for the weekend, all those arriving were marked with a stamp. This went smoothly until the boss decided to have a go. After chatting to the occupants of the second car he realised they had driven off with the stamp, which he had absent-mindedly left on the car roof. He was immediately banned from "helping" at the gate.

Those who came were not disappointed. As well as a full and varied programme in the Children's Area, theatre and cinema marquees, and speakers like Bruce Kent, E.P. Thompson and Sir George Trevelyan, the crowd were treated to first class entertainers on the new Pyramid Stage. These included John Cooper Clarke, Roy Harper and Ginger Baker on Friday, Aswad, New Order and Hawkwind on Saturday, and Talisman, Taj Mahal and Gordon Gilltrap on Sunday — all introduced by Radio 1 disc jockey Pete Drummond. Patrice Warrener's laser show rounded things off beautifully.

As satisfied customers made their way home, compliments were received from the police, the local authority, and the Samaritans who called it "a well organised and together festival". About £20,000 was eventually handed over to a very grateful CND by Michael Eavis, who made this comment to the local paper. "I am absolutely delighted with the way things went. It was like putting a coin in a one-armed bandit and watching the jackpot appear in each window — everything turned out just as we wanted it."

One sunny July afternoon a small group of people from the local planning department visited Worthy Farm to examine the recently constructed cowshed. They found the stage piled high with hay and a herd of friendly Friesians gathered around to show off their new winter quarters.

Following a thorough examination of the structure, in order to confirm that it was a safe place for cows to shelter in and bands to play on, they agreed the Pyramid could stay, and even commented on how beautiful it looked.

However, because of his late application for permission to build the "cowshed", Michael was fined £215 plus costs.

And so, thanks to Cheops, Tony Andrews of Turbosound, Ian, Roger, John and the tireless band of pyramid builders, and understanding planners, the Pyramid was here, and here to stay.

1982 18th to 20th June

SUMMERTIME IN ENGLAND

This was the first year National CND were involved in running the Gate. Dan Plesch and Pat Wilson from West of England CND had been to the previous year's festival when they had helped in the CND marquee, and arranged the showing of "The War Game". In 1982, however, Michael asked them to take over control of the Main Gate and the Traders' Gate. It was their responsibility to make sure that site entrances were manned at all times, day and night. At the Main Entrance tickets were bought and sold, and given up in exchange for an indellible mark which was stamped on the backs of thousands of hands. Here wrangles went on between the Gate people and punters, who, having left their tickets/passes/ money, etc. at home, still tried to gain admission to the site. At the Traders' Gate there was a different set of problems, all just as difficult to sort out.

For most of the year the farm tracks have only to cope with the passage of tractors and other farm vehicles, but to withstand the heavy volume of festival traffic, and to allow ready access to emergency vehicles, something more substantial was needed, and in the weeks before the festival began, lorry load after lorry load of hardcore from local quarries was laid along the main tracks to form hard and durable roads.

Once again Mark Cann helped to organise the Information stall, and in addition to this he took charge of liaison between backstage and the rest of the site. By the end of the festival Mark had become a key person in the smooth running of the back stage area, and from then on it has been his job to ensure that all the bands needs are catered for, and all their contract requirements met — however bizarre. For instance when Steel Pulse insisted on a special Rastafarian meal consisting of fresh snapper fish (scales and all), sweet potatoes and plantains, Mark explained that these were impossible to get in Shepton Mallet. However, when their road manager arrived with all the required ingredients in a carrier bag, Mark arranged for these to be prepared in the back stage kitchen.

More about what goes on back-stage later.

This was also the year when Mid-Somerset CND took overall charge of Information. They were the people to go to not only to find out when your favourite band would be playing and where the nearest pay phones were, but also for help in planning your journey home, with bus and train timetables.

If you came, you will remember that '82 was a muddy festival.

On the Friday it rained. It rained very hard and for a long time. In the Market Area, the main thoroughfares were soon transformed into strips of oozing mud. The brolly stalls and wellie sellers did a roaring trade — and those with an eye for making a bob or two hurried along to the nearest town, bought up their stocks of rubber boots and sold them on site to those in need who didn't care how much they paid just for the luxury of clean, dry feet!

John Cooper Clarke was first to appear on stage on Friday afternoon, and later on top reggae band Black Uhuru got the crowd dancing in the pouring rain.

Incidentally it was the wettest day in Somerset for 45 years.

By Saturday the rain had stopped, but Friday's cloudburst had turned the site into a quagmire. Still, it was possible to get around, and with the improvement in weather conditions the stallholders brought out their colourful array of wares and the whole site came back to life. All around were beautifully crafted wooden toys, jewellery, ponchos and wall hangings from South America, records, shoes, mystical books, rainbow coloured candles, and tinkling brass wind-chimes dancing in the unexpected sunshine. Further on a cheerful confusion of stallholders vied for the food trade, offering the exotic and the plain.

The African dance group Ekome got the show on the road on Saturday afternoon, and then came one of the guest speakers, E.P. Thompson.

As usual, this veteran of peace rallies gave an inspiring and clear sighted speech about the whole nuclear issue. Everyone listened — the punks, the bikers, the die-hard hippies, all gave E.P. the attention he demanded, the attention he deserved.

Surprise guest Roy Harper was next on stage, and he began with a song dedicated to Worthy Farm called "Mushroom Valley", and got the crowds holding hands and joining in. A very pleasant set.

It was by this time around 4 o'clock and the late afternoon sun was hanging low in the sky over Glastonbury Tor. A breeze had got up — and it hadn't rained for hours. The crowd in the arena grew as from the surrounding hillsides more and more people moved steadily towards the stage.

It was time . . .

Van Morrison shuffled onto the stage, hardly noticing the crowds. A man totally absorbed in what he was doing — no niceties here. Much of his performance featured new songs from his recently released "Beautiful Vision" album, but the high spot of the set was the intensely moving "Summertime in England". For here we all were, standing in those very fields about which Van the Man was singing. Eighty minutes later the crowd reluctantly let him go, but not before bringing him back for a final rousing encore of "Gloria".

On Sunday afternoon a light aircraft trailing a giant banner with the slogan "Help the Soviets. Support CND" flew over Worthy Farm. Suddenly two rockets exploded behind it and the aircraft turned tail and disappeared.

The rockets, costing £70 each, had been intended for that evening's firework and laser display, but Michael Eavis thought they could be put to better use! Several weeks later the pilot appeared in a local court and was convicted of low flying and fined £400. He has not been seen since.

Later, the Bishop of Bath and Wells visited the site, and addressed his temporary flock from the Main Stage. He stayed afterwards and spoke to many of the festival-goers individually.

Sunday's Main Stage line-up was dominated by two American performers. Jackson Browne who has long been an active supporter of the anti-nuclear movement, re-scheduled his European tour to appear at Glastonbury, so important was it to him to be part of this peace festival.

At the end of the evening, Richie Havens topped the bill, and those who had stayed on to see him were well rewarded by his predictably outstanding performance. He is a hardened campaigner who has devoted much of his life to the cause of racial equality and world peace.

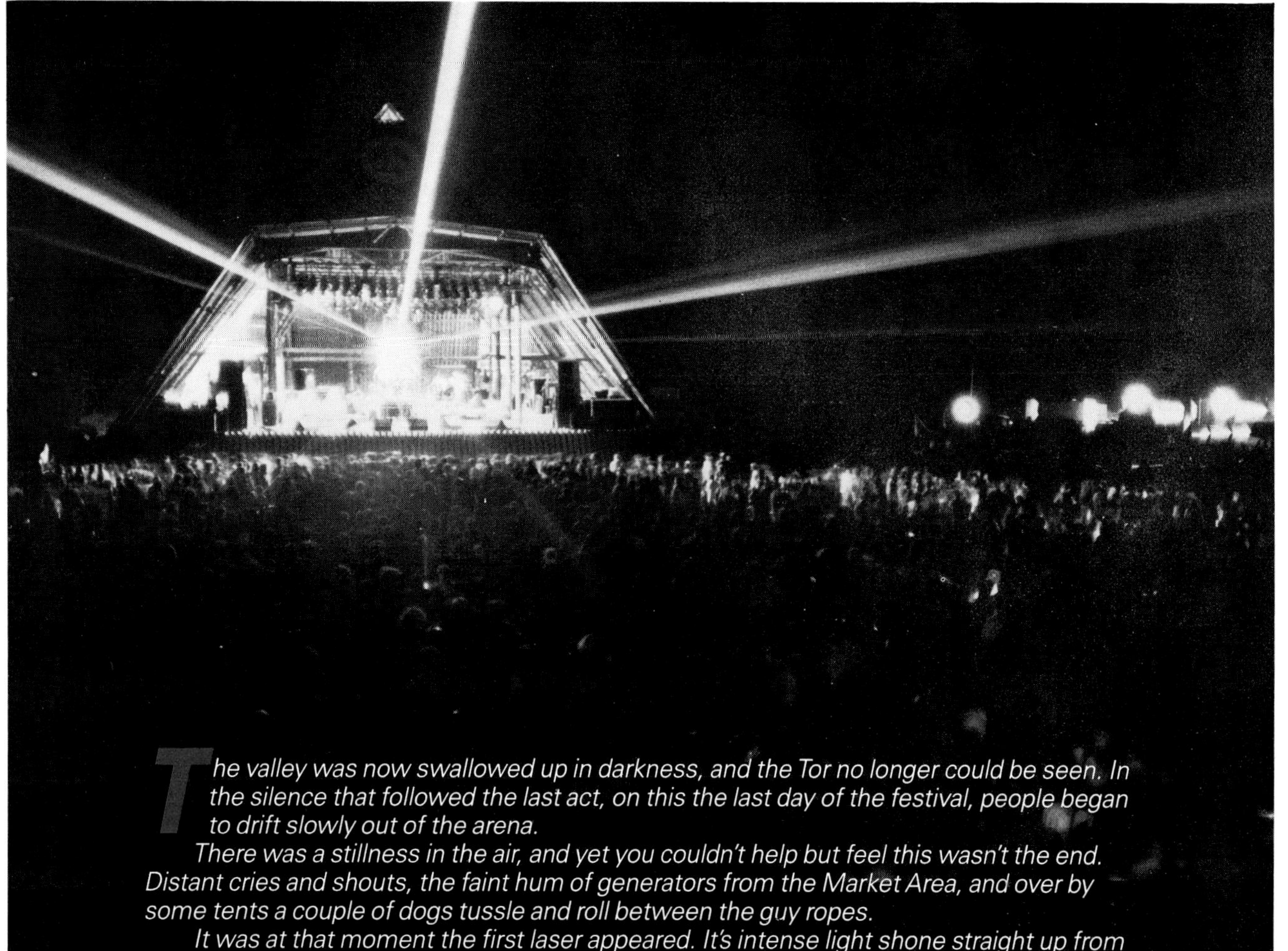

The valley was now swallowed up in darkness, and the Tor no longer could be seen. In the silence that followed the last act, on this the last day of the festival, people began to drift slowly out of the arena.

There was a stillness in the air, and yet you couldn't help but feel this wasn't the end. Distant cries and shouts, the faint hum of generators from the Market Area, and over by some tents a couple of dogs tussle and roll between the guy ropes.

It was at that moment the first laser appeared. It's intense light shone straight up from the Pyramid — earth's energies being transmitted upward ('82 style!) towards the sky. Strange electronic sounds were emitted from the speakers — Gary Numan and his Tubeway Army asking "Are Friends Electric?" The beam arched its way down to touch the top of Home Ground, and the farmhouse. Then, almost imperceptively, it crept along the northern ridge of hills, finally coming to rest on the Tor itself.

This was just the beginning of the most amazing laser show we've ever seen at Glastonbury. Modern technology and ancient earth forces working together. Glastonbury is the very heart of England, and wonderful things were happening here — and would for many years to come.

GLASTONBURY
CND FESTIVAL 1983
MEDICAL CREW
GLASTONBURY
CND FESTIVAL 1983
WORTHY FARM, PILTON, SHEPTON MALLET, SOMERSET.
GATE
STAFF

GLASTONBURY
CND FESTIVAL 1983
WORTHY FARM, PILTON, SHEPTON MALLET, SOMERSET.
17th.18th.19th. JUNE. WORTHY FARM, PILTON, SHEPTON MALLET, SOMERSET.
Three-Day Advance Ticket - £12-00
Camping, Car-parking, V.A.T. and all On-Site Events are included in the ticket price.
№ 2954
GLASTONBURY
CND FESTIVAL 1983
ACCESS
ALL
AREAS
GLASTONBURY
CND FESTIVAL 1983
THEATRE

ENDLESS SUNSHINE

As preparations got underway for the 1983 Festival, it was clear that this year a licence would have to be obtained. Since the previous year's festival the Local Government (Miscellaneous Provisions) Act had become law, giving local authorities the power to regulate such events by stipulating conditions which had to be met. The licence which Mendip District Council eventually issued set a crowd limit of 30,000 and went into considerable detail about access roads, water supply, loos and so on. There had always been very close co-operation between Michael Eavis and all the authorities concerned, but where this had previously taken place informally, now it all became much more official.

As the festivals have grown from year to year, different groups of people have taken on responsibility for running certain aspects of it. 1983 was the year that National CND involved itself in a big way organising Gate and Traffic, employing CND members from groups all over the country. Nick and Mandy Scholefield of the local Mid-Somerset CND group took charge of Information operating from a circular tent in one corner of the site. Another recruit this year was Henri Otani, a cybernetics specialist who had arrived with friends in '82 and set up an impromptu communications system with walkie-talkies. They were invited back officially in '83 and have been responsible for keeping everyone in touch ever since, an often thankless task which involves a great deal of hard work and long hours.

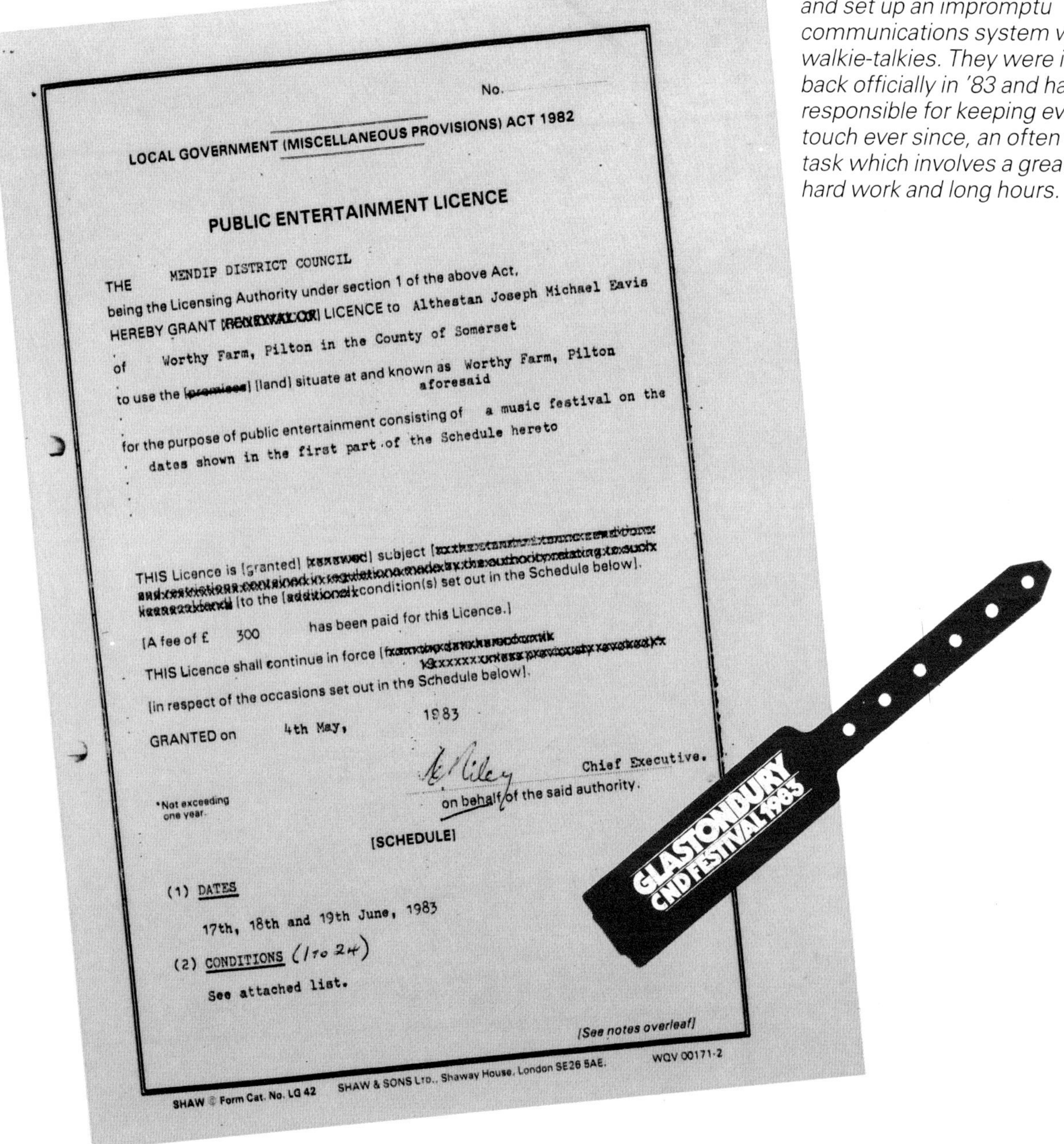

No.

LOCAL GOVERNMENT (MISCELLANEOUS PROVISIONS) ACT 1982

PUBLIC ENTERTAINMENT LICENCE

THE MENDIP DISTRICT COUNCIL
being the Licensing Authority under section 1 of the above Act,
HEREBY GRANT LICENCE to Althestan Joseph Michael Eavis
of Worthy Farm, Pilton in the County of Somerset
to use the [land] situate at and known as Worthy Farm, Pilton aforesaid
for the purpose of public entertainment consisting of a music festival on the dates shown in the first part of the Schedule hereto

THIS Licence is [granted] subject [to the condition(s) set out in the Schedule below].

[A fee of £ 300 has been paid for this Licence.]

THIS Licence shall continue in force [in respect of the occasions set out in the Schedule below].

GRANTED on 4th May, 1983

Chief Executive.
on behalf of the said authority.

*Not exceeding one year.

[SCHEDULE]

(1) DATES

17th, 18th and 19th June, 1983

(2) CONDITIONS (1 to 24)

See attached list.

[See notes overleaf]

SHAW © Form Cat. No. LG 42 SHAW & SONS Ltd., Shaway House, London SE26 5AE. WQV 00171-2

The Children's Area drew praise from many quarters. The local paper called it a "Paradise for Children" with the comment that "Donkey rides, climbing frames, swings and a model railway circuit would bring a smile to any child's face. Add to these the inflatables, the aerial runway, the clowns, theatre, face-painting and the endless sunshine, it was heaven on earth for the young."

Theatre grew to maturity from its small scale beginnings with a non-stop programme in two marquees. From noon to 3 am there was music and mime, comedy and dance. Rik Mayall was there, and so was Nigel Planer. There were the Flying Pickets and the Ekome dance troupe. Zippo the Clown, Jamie McGruther and Professor Panic entertained the kids and grown-ups alike. Meanwhile Brides Against the Bomb reminded us why we were all there.

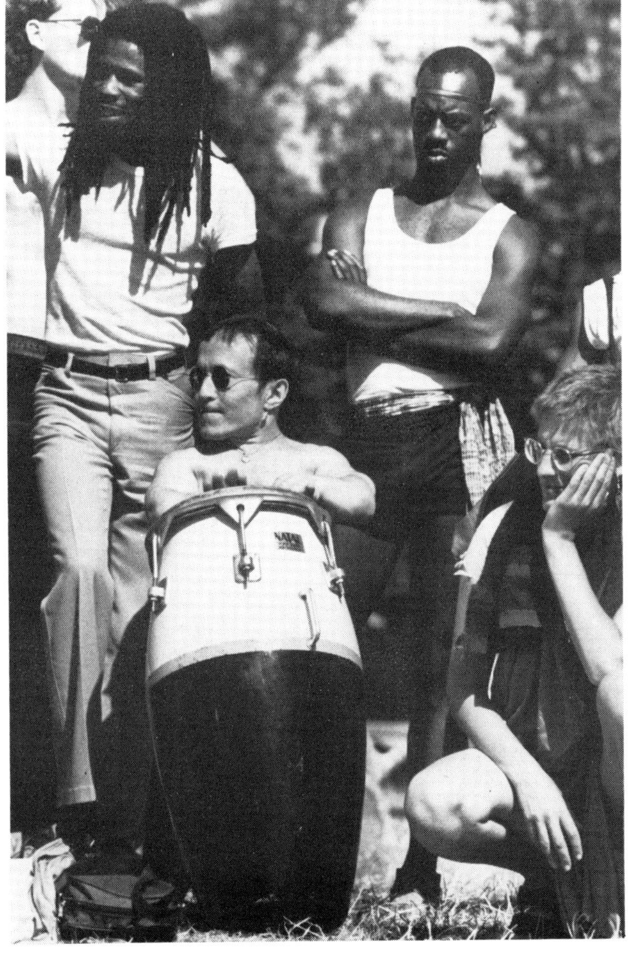

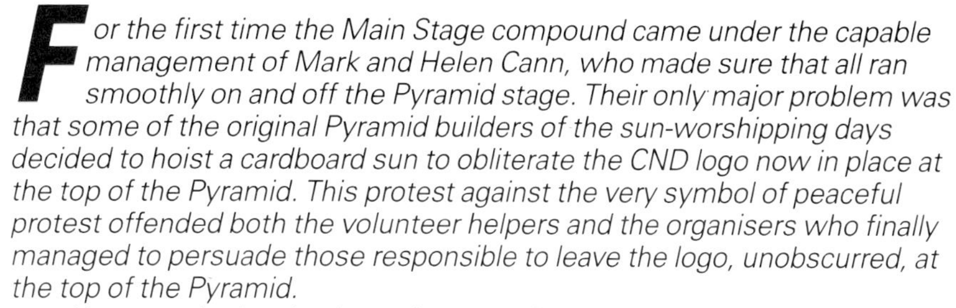

For the first time the Main Stage compound came under the capable management of Mark and Helen Cann, who made sure that all ran smoothly on and off the Pyramid stage. Their only major problem was that some of the original Pyramid builders of the sun-worshipping days decided to hoist a cardboard sun to obliterate the CND logo now in place at the top of the Pyramid. This protest against the very symbol of peaceful protest offended both the volunteer helpers and the organisers who finally managed to persuade those responsible to leave the logo, unobscurred, at the top of the Pyramid.

However, in the sky the real sun continued to grace the Festival and gradually as the weekend progressed the exposed bodies acquired a tan if you were careful, or became burnt if you were not. Gallons of calamine lotion were applied to sore red flesh at the Medical Centre, and Hay Fever was at its peak.

Comperes Johnnie Walker, Alexis Korner and Alexei Sayle introduced Jean-Philippe Rykiel, Marillion and Melanie on Friday; Tom Paxton, The Enid, The Beat, Aswad and UB40 — the highlight of the day — on Saturday. But it was generally agreed that the glorious weather on Sunday brought out the best on the stage. The haunting South American melodies of Incantation, the traditional Irish jigs of the Chieftains, the bitter-sweet pop of Fun Boy Three and the superb, compelling vocals of Curtis Mayfield. The greatest delight came with the contemporary ju-ju music of King Sunny Adé which provided the finalé. Undisputed leader of ju-ju, Sunny Adé had the crowd dancing from beginning to end. As he said, "Ju-ju music is party music" and what an end of festival party everyone had!*

1983 was regarded as a success by many people including some Pilton villagers who began to complain not about its existence, but that it had become known as the Glastonbury and not the Pilton CND Festival! Others set up stalls in their gardens, providing sandwiches, pies and teas for the festival people, since there were no other off-site facilities in the village.

The local authority chief commented that there had been remarkably few problems on or off the site considering the numbers involved and that "Mr. Eavis had made considerable efforts to comply with regulations" although the 30,000 limit had been exceeded. Michael himself was quoted as saying "I think we have reached a peak now. It is an incredibly successful venture."

But the last word on 1983 must go to Phil Gray of the Shepton Mallet Journal who wrote — "The Festival was after all a sun-blessed success for Michael Eavis, CND, the artistes, and not least the crowd. Bringing together the complex kaleidoscope of musical and artistic talent was no mean feat, and Somerset in particular should be grateful it can be achieved and hopefully can be achieved again. To do this, everyone must be kept happy — and that includes all at Worthy Farm, local residents and the local authorities."

EIGHTY PENCE
1984
PROGRAMME
MUSIC
THEATRE
CABARET
CINEMA
CHILDRENS WORLD
CAMPAIGN
SPEAKERS
LISTINGS
GLASTONBURY C.N.D. FESTIVAL
22ND: 23RD & 24TH OF JUNE 1984
WORTHY FARM: PILTON: SHEPTON MALLET
SOMERSET: ENGLAND
OFFICIAL PROGRAMME

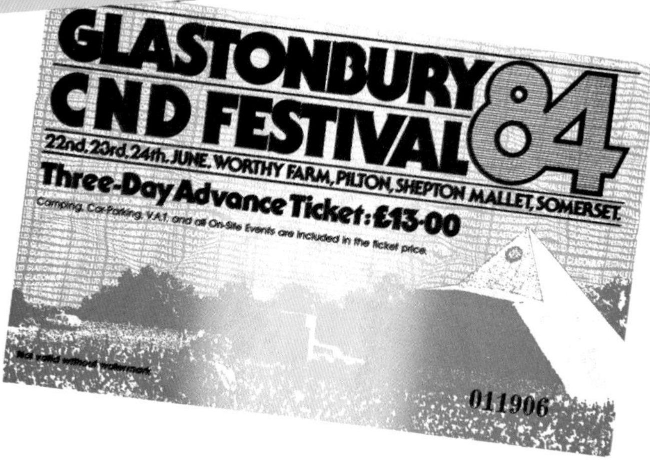
GLASTONBURY CND FESTIVAL 84
22nd. 23rd. 24th. JUNE. WORTHY FARM, PILTON, SHEPTON MALLET, SOMERSET.
Three-Day Advance Ticket: £13-00
Camping, Car-Parking, V.A.T. and all On-Site Events are included in the ticket price.
011906

NO CRUISE – PEACE

Vol. CXXX – No. 3

Pilton festival promoter wins in court case

MICHAEL EAVIS, promoter of the celebrated Glastonbury ... on his Worthy Farm at Pilton, has successfully ... prosecutions brought by Mendip District ... contraventions of five of the 24 ... licensed to stage last

PRESS, THURSDAY, JANUARY 19, 1984

Pop farmer plans record festival

By Paul Stokes

FARMER Michael Eavis is planning to stage the biggest-ever three-day pop festival on his Somerset site this year.

He was cleared by Shepton Mallet magistrates on Tuesday of five alleged breaches of condition at last year's festival which attracted some 30,000 people.

Mendip district council brought the prosecution which was the first of its kind under new festival licensing laws.

Any conviction could have been used to block the granting of a licence for future festivals at Mr Eavis's Worthy Farm, Pilton, near Shepton Mallet.

But last night he said: "They have no grounds to refuse the licence. We will be applying for this year's in April and hope to get permission for a 35,000 crowd.

"We have been working at it for a long time now. We are expanding all facilities and entertainments for this year's festival."

The mid-summer festival, which will take place starting on June 22 this year, will be the eighth to held at Worthy Fa...

The first was held in ... and attracted 2,000 people.

In the past three ... 12,000, 22,000 and ... 30,000 have been on th... val site.

During the last thr...

the festival has raised £133,000 for CND.

Mr Eavis said in addition last year £3,000 went to local charities and even he hoped more would go to local causes in future years.

He said CND would not always necessarily be the major beneficiary from the proceeds.

The chairman of Mendip district council's Environmental Health committee Councillor Clifford Perkins, last night expressed his "dis...", over Mr Eavis's acquittal.

Councillor Perkins' ... issued the ... under the ...

the committee considered reports from the police, fire authority and health department on alleged breaches and, on the recommendation of the police agreed that Mr Eavis should be prosecuted for five breaches including the breaking of the 30,000 attendance limit.

Mr Eavis's defence was that he had taken all reasonable steps to comply with the conditions.

Had the case been found proved he could have been fined up to £1,000. Instead the magistrates dismissed all the summonses.

Councillor Perkins said: "I was disgusted by the verdict. What is the point in a council imposing conditions if they can be broken without even a ...inal penalty?

Farmer Eavis can keep on rocking

MR MICHAEL Eavis, organiser of last summer's Pilton CND rock festival, was cleared of breaking his site licence conditions by Shepton Mallet magistrates yesterday.

Five alleged breaches brought against Mr Eavis, of Worthy Farm, Pilton, by Mendip district council were dismissed at a unique hearing.

It was the first prosecution of its kind since new licensing legislation was introduced early last year.

The council's senior environmental health officer, Mr David Burton, said the festival attendance had exceeded the agreed 30,000 limit, the admissions system had failed and some emergency exits were blocked.

There was a lack of hard surfaces on the site and no exclusive telephone for emergency use.

Mr Eavis, denying the allegations, said attendance did not exceed the limit though some tickets had been forged.

Shepton Mallet GP, Dr Chris Howes, who ran the medical services during the festival, said arrangements were extremely good and emergency services had encountered no problems.

Mr David Wood, defending, said Mendip should count itself fortunate having such a successful organisation running the festival.

Michael Eavis

...y Otani, of Bath, the ... liaison officer, said ... an exclusive telephone ... he was not aware of any ...ator failures that meant the ...could not be used.

The prosecution ... said that Mr. Eavis was co-operative and helpful, an... Wood asked the magistrates ... give him the benefit of the doubt.

The prosecution witnesses called by Mendip Council's solicitor, Mr. Graham Jeffs, were Chief Inspector Tony Pink, Fire Officer Keith Furlonger and Environmental Health Officer Mr. David Burton, an acknowledged

... and that ... had been "foisted ...

Mr. Eavis told ... that the organisers had dis...red 640 forged tickets which had been handed to the police. It was

This was the eighth midsummer music festival held at Worthy Farm, attended by an estimated 50,000 people. Once against the Campaign for Nuclear Disarmament benefitted, and the large donation made could not have been more timely in the aftermath of the deployment of American Cruise missiles in Britain.

In January 1984 Michael Eavis successfully defended five prosecutions brought against him by Mendip District Council alleging contraventions of the previous year's licence conditions. All five charges were dismissed after a day-long hearing at Shepton Mallet Magistrates Court, and soon afterwards plans were under way for the biggest ever three-day festival to be held at Worthy Farm the following June. Once again a licence was obtained which this time stipulated a crowd limit of 35,000.

Car parking had always been a problem. At the earlier festivals attended by much smaller numbers, people had simply been shown onto the site and left to find their own place to park and camp. This had resulted in very haphazard parking, with vehicles and tents jumbled together across the site, often obstructing the roadways. With more people and vehicles than ever expected, chaos seemed inevitable if this policy were allowed to continue.

It was decided that specific parking areas should be designated, and stewards employed to direct traffic to them. For the most part camping and parking would be segregated, though in a few fields camping alongside vehicles would be allowed. This pleased the fire chief, who had been concerned about the fire risk created by mixing camping and parking.

The PTA of nearby West Pennard School took on the task of providing stewards. They had a tough job persuading people to park only in certain areas, when they had perhaps been stuck in traffic jams for several hours waiting to get onto the site. With so many cars continually pouring through the main gate, it was difficult to sort out the problems of individual drivers and the system failed on many occasions. Pilton villager John Wheat who was in charge of the operation said it was like "striving to control anarchy" at times. Nevertheless, they kept traffic moving and managed to persuade most people to park sensibly.

The result was remarkable.

By Friday evening all the parking areas were full, and Michael arranged for overspill fields to be opened up on neighbouring farms. Messages were broadcast on radio that unless you had a three-day advance ticket you should turn round and go home again. "Site Full" signs went up on the main gate, but still the fans arrived in their thousands.

In exchange for their ticket people were issued at the gate with pink wrist bands, which were clipped on and could only be removed by cutting. An exception was made in the case of children who might have been injured if the bands had become caught up in play area apparatus. Council officials carrying out a head count noticed that not everyone on site was wearing one of these bands. Michael admitted that however good their security system there were bound to be infiltrators, and indeed that at one point police trying to cope with traffic congestion off site had asked him to admit people without tickets.

Undoubtedly the attendance limit was exceeded over the weekend. Local councillors felt that the festival had now reached its natural peak and that it would make sense to increase the limit to 50,000 next time, provided that the organisers could lay on adequate facilities for this number. Incidentally this would enable them to raise the cost of the licence to £2000!

This year the organisers decided to make a stand against the blatant sale of illegal drugs on site. They posted warning notices informing the festival goers that the sale and display of drugs were forbidden, and launched their own undercover anti-drugs operation, removing signs put up by drug touts and trying to persuade them to desist.

In the event, illegal drugs caused fewer problems than alcohol. One or two scuffles broke out in the Arena between people who had been indulging in too much of the local beer and cider. Because of this Michael decided to put a limit on alcohol sales the following year, saying at the time, "Some people aren't into music, CND or improving the world. They just come along to whoop it up and have a drink. Although there wasn't a lot of drunkenness, it destroyed the spirit of the festival and lowered the tone."

On the whole, festival goers are well able to look after themselves, but sometimes problems arise. In the course of less than a week, a vast shanty town of tents, campers, caravans, and make-shift shelters springs up, provides a temporary home for a huge population, and disappears. The sheer volume of people crowded together, close to open fires, gas cylinders and overhead power cables, or tramping backwards and forwards from one part of the site to another — inevitably some have accidents, some become ill. Emergency routes have to be kept clear, all parts of the site must remain accessible. Ambulances and fire engines must be able to get on and off the site unimpeded.

At the end of the festival, medical co-ordinator Dr. Chris Howes was exhausted but relieved that everything had been coped with reasonably well. There had been some worrying moments. A gas cylinder explosion which had destroyed in seconds the tent in which a family of four were settling down for the night; on that occasion the casualties had been rescued and resuscitated and were in the burns unit at Bristol within 90 minutes. A man who had tried to take his life by severing an artery with a pair of scissors had needed two simultaneous intravenous infusions and the efforts of a doctor and nurse all the way to hospital in Bath to keep him alive.

But everyone had survived, there had been no disasters, and as Chris said, for three days in the year, there is nowhere safer to be in the whole of Somerset than Worthy Farm!

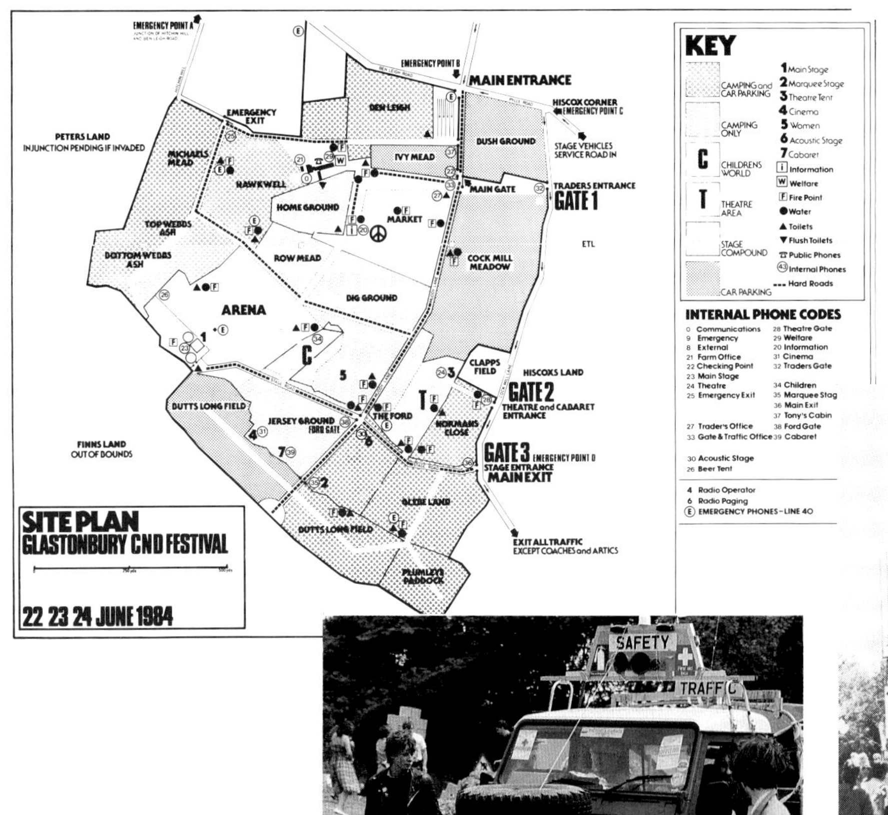

Once more the Pyramid stage presented an outstanding and varied line up. On Friday Billy Bragg armed with no more than a scratchy electric guitar and a collection of characteristically bitter sweet lyrics reached out across the valley.

Also that afternoon American folk singer Joan Baez sang. Back in the '60s she had taken the folk world by storm with her thrilling lush voice, promoting the work of writers such as Phil Ochs and Bob Dylan. But music was never enough, and gradually she became a symbol of opposition to all that was unjust in America and the world. Her support for peace and human rights was always non-violent and she was instrumental in establishing Amnesty International in America. Twenty years on her voice, as clear and compelling as ever, seemed to reawaken memories of the first Worthy Farm festival.

"Disarmament we look upon as an issue absolutely included in human rights, because the right to remain alive is the basic human right."
Joan Baez

It was eight o'clock and great to see Ian Dury again. The crowds responded to his tight and raw-edged performance, as he spat with venom the words of "Spasticus Autisticus" — his musical contribution to the Year of the Disabled 1982. His superb backing group provided a firm funky base for old favourites like "Wake Up" and "What a Waste".

On Saturday one of the guest speakers was Paddy Ashdown, Liberal MP for Yeovil, and, at that time, an unusually outspoken supporter of nuclear disarmament. He said one of the greatest speeches ever was that made by Lord Louis Mountbatten just a few days before he was murdered when he said that "mankind now stood on the edge of the final abyss".

"I believe that is exactly where we are" said Mr. Ashdown, "so I say to you it is not good enough just to blame the politicians for putting us there — though goodness knows they have blame enough to carry . . . . Worst of all is the prophecy we hold over the generations which follow us, and that is a prophecy of desolation, a prophecy of a broken humanity, and a prophecy above all of a visitation of a plague of mis-shapen children. It is our duty and our responsibility to rid the world in which we stand of that terrible legacy".

Also on stage that afternoon were the popular young reggae band Amazulu. Devoted to breaking down musical barriers, Amazulu draw on a far-reaching background of cultures with members of their six piece band from such wide ranging places as South Africa, Belize, Brazil, Liverpool and London. Their lively and happy set pleased the crowds.

Following straight on came Dublin based band The Waterboys. Formed by Mike Scott in 1982 their popularity has grown steadily, and they recently joined the Pretenders on their European tour. Their energetic set included tracks from their newly released album "A Pagan Place", and the crowd loved them.

At six o'clock the Smiths strolled onto the stage to a wild reception from their waiting fans. This unpretentious and charming band had been voted Best New Act of 1983, following the success of their first single "Hand in Glove". During their set they sang several numbers from "The Smiths" album, as well as two favourites "What difference does it make" and "Heaven knows I'm miserable now".

Later on that evening six members of the General Public walked onto the Pyramid stage and proceeded to delight the crowds with a selection from their recently released self-named album. Heading the line up were two ex-Beat vocalists Dave Wakelin and Ranking Roger.

Bruce Kent — General Secretary of CND — was guest speaker on Sunday, and gave a rousing address. He ended his speech by calling for a round of appreciation for the man who had opened up his farm for the benefit of humanity.

It was great to see veteran rock band Fairport Convention back in action again at Glastonbury, and that night American jazz/rock group Weather Report played to the crowds.

African singer Fela Kuti topped the bill and as the time drew close to when he was due to appear, the crowds gathered from all corners of the site. He has been described as the ultimate rebel, politically outspoken and unwavering, and certainly the most controversial African musician currently active, accusing politicians of being corrupt and over laden with hypocrisy. He is also a brilliant song writer, singer and saxophonist who has unequalled stage presence. With numbers such as "V.I.P. Vagabonds in Power", and "I.T.T. International Thief Thief", he was perhaps the most thought provoking booking of the weekend.

CND

PRESS INFORMATION
GLASTONBURY
CND FESTIVAL 1985
Friday 21st Saturday 22nd Sunday 23rd June
PASS 1985 PASS
GATE
GLASTONBURY CND · FESTIVAL
PASS 1985 PASS
THEATRE
GLASTONBURY CND · FESTIVAL
PASS 1985 PASS
KIDS
GLASTONBURY CND · FESTIVAL
PASS 1985 PASS
ON STAGE
GLASTONBURY
PASS 1985 PASS
CABARET
PASS 1985 PASS
PRESS
Publication
GLASTONBURY CND · FESTIVAL
PASS 1985 PASS
BACK STAGE
GLASTONBURY
PASS 1985 PASS
INFORMATION
GLASTONBURY CND · FESTIVAL
PASS 1985 PASS
ACOUSTIC STAGE
GLASTONBURY CND · FESTIVAL
PASS 1985 PASS
GLASTONBURY CND · FESTIVAL
PASS 1985 PASS
WELFARE
GLASTONBURY CND · FESTIVAL
Glastonbury Festivals Ltd. Registered Office: Worthy Farm, Pilton, Somerset. V.A.T. No: 397 37367 89

SINGING IN THE RAIN

As the festival grew bigger year by year, it seemed inevitable that the time would come when Worthy Farm would be too small to accommodate it. Indeed in 1984 the site had begun to feel somewhat overcrowded. So it was timely that early in 1985 a neighbouring farm unexpectedly came onto the market. Cockmill Farm enlarged the site by a further 100 acres.

Over the years the festival has gained the respect of those in the music business, and established a reputation as one of the leading events of its kind in the whole of Europe. Some of the biggest names in the business were approached to appear on the Main Stage, and confirmation of bookings soon came in from The Style Council, Echo and the Bunnymen, Colour Field, The Pogues, The Boomtown Rats and Joe Cocker, as well as the welcome return of Alexei Sayle, Billy Bragg, Ian Dury and the Blockheads, and Roger Chapman who had appeared on the first pyramid stage back in 1971, when he was the singer with Family.

Hopes were high as the solstice approached that this would be the biggest and the best yet. Then, on Thursday 20th June it started to rain . . .

25,000 people were already on site — 20,000 more were due to arrive at any time — would the organisation stand up in the rapidly deteriorating conditions? Michael was sure that it would and somehow his confidence spread around the site.

The expected crowds continued to arrive. Some had taken note of the weather forecasts and came suitably equipped, but others turned up totally unprepared for the conditions. As in 1982, the enterprising market traders cleaned up on the wellie and brolly scene. Dustbin liners with holes cut out for the head and arms made inexpensive plastic macs and body warmers, and these were handed out free to anyone who made it up the slippery hill to Welfare.

The Medical and Welfare teams spent much of their time rescuing some of those who had come least prepared, and who arrived cold, wet and miserable on their doorstep. Soon the Wagon Shed next to the farmhouse was full of shivering bodies wrapped in blankets, and huddled in front of electric fires, while their sodden clothes were at least partly dried out. The Safety vehicles patroiling the site picked up a number of casualties suffering from exposure and hypothermia. Several of these were drunk, lying unconscious and face-down in the mud — in real danger. To everyone's great relief they all survived.

The sheer size of the newly enlarged site meant that communications were stretched to the limit. The radio telephones suffered badly from interference and although everyone was supposed to keep them in plastic bags, the rain eventually seeped inside the casings, causing some to pack up altogether. Vehicles became hopelessly stuck in the rapidly enlarging muddy lake produced by 80,000 trudging feet. Walking anywhere was an adventure at best and a nightmare at worst, since most of the site is on a hill — wonderful as an amphitheatre, but not so good at times like these.

This really was the ultimate test for the organisation.

To escape the rain many more people than usual looked to the marquee entertainments. Unfortunately marquees crammed to overflowing with soaking wet people tend to generate a good deal of heat, the heat turns the moisture to steam which rises to the canvas roof, condenses and falls as rain on the hapless audiences. Soon it was almost as wet inside as out!

Patience and tempers could easily have snapped, desperation could easily have set in. But the Glastonbury spirit is strong, Reporters likened the scene to a refugee camp or Dunkirk — irony indeed considering the number of committed pacifists involved. It occurred to more than a few that conditions far worse than these would prevail should the nuclear holocaust ever become reality. The words of the old campaign song came to mind, this time with new meaning — "We shall overcome".

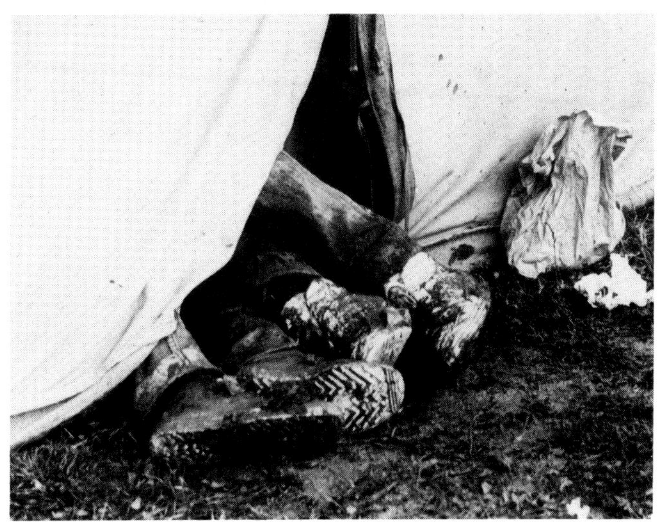

Meanwhile the weather was causing problems for the backstage crew. With twenty bands due to play over the three days, each needing access for their Starliner coaches and heavy trucks, it was obvious by Friday morning that the stage road, by now rapidly disappearing under the mud, would soon be impassable. A new hard road was the only answer. Helen Cann got to work ringing round the local quarries, and before long truckloads of roadstone began to appear, followed by heavy rollers to level it all out, and by the time the first bands arrived, the new road was ready.

Later on that afternoon, and just a matter of weeks before the incredible Live Aid concert, the Boomtown Rats appeared on the Main Stage, and proved the high spot of the day's line-up. They delighted the crowd with old favourites like "Mondays", "Rat Trap" and "Never in a Million Years", together with material from the "In the Long Grass" album. Unfortunately, what can only be described as drunken frustration with the weather led to a bout of mud throwing. But Bob Geldof, whose main concern seemed to be for his clean white WHAM! T-shirt, gave verbally as good as he got, pointing out that this was supposed to be a festival about peace and love. The mud throwing stopped.

"Blessed are the peacemakers — not just those who live in peace. We cannot dis-invent nuclear weapons. But we can invent a new community of mankind to see that they are banished from the earth."

Bruce Kent.

On Saturday, Aswad and Midnight Oil tried hard to lift the spirits of the crowd in the drizzle, helped along by Alexei Sayle who told the crowd at one point "I don't know why you don't all go home!", and later gave out what he called a very important announcement: "Someone has lost a contact lens out there". Groans from the arena. Then Style Council gave a very polished performance. Paul Weller is well known for his anti-nuclear convictions so it was particularly pleasing to see his band at Glastonbury even though they did have the nerve to play "Long Hot Summer". Then at around 11 pm everyone really had a reason to be cheerful — the welcome return of Ian Dury, together again with the Blockheads. He too was on the receiving end of some of the squelchy stuff, causing him to leave the stage for a while. Eventually he came back and roused us all with "Sweet Gene Vincent", "Rhythmn Stick", and "Sex and Drugs and Rock'n'Roll". We forgot the rain.

The Sunday line-up was particularly strong and varied — Billy Bragg, Clannad, Colour Field, and Echo and the Bunnymen. Then a long wait in the pouring rain. Ankle deep in mud we watched the stage made ready for the legendary Joe Cocker. The wait was worth it. After being away for so long, Cocker was back just as we remembered him, his power and presence undiminished. "Delta Lady" and "With a Little Help from my Friends" had never sounded so good.

WORKING WEEK/THE UNTOUCHABLES/MIDNIGHT OIL/THE STYLE COUNCIL

GLASTONBURY: CND FESTIVAL

MUD: it's what you get if 40,000 people tramp around a small farm for 48 hours in almost constant rain. A *lot* of mud.

By Saturday, the second day of three, Glastonbury Festival looks a lot more like a refugee camp than a really "fun" place to be – thousands of sodden tents in a sea of oozing, squelching, splashing, horrible *mud.* And, for that matter, the crowd look more like a bunch of prisoners of war than people on a weekend's holiday.

The sensible ones have brought wellies and waterproofs; the less prudent have done their best with plastic bags, putting them on their heads, on their feet, over their t-shirts. *Very* elegant.

Mind you, there *is* a lot to see. In small marquee tents you can get a glimpse of every imaginable type of "alternative" performer – jugglers, acrobats, mime artists, conjurers, comics, folk singers, poets and more. And from the hundreds of stalls you can buy hand-painted beads, hand-made pottery, hand-printed cloth, hand-made sandals, not to mention the Indian incense sticks that seem to be everywhere.

In amongst the chip vans, hippies offer you strange looking soya burgers for 50p, and *yes*, there really *is* someone selling lentil soup, served from a huge and dodgy-looking bubbling pot.

But the biggest gathering is around the main stage, a bizarre grey pyramid bearing a large white CND symbol to remind you of the cause to which you've donated most of your £16 (!) entrance fee.

As the jazzy Working Week leave the stage the rain gets even harder. ("Wow man, this is getting really heaveee.") Replacing them, The Untouchables do their best to lift the gloom, bounding around wildly on the raised platform, and some members of the crowd respond by flinging themselves about in the mud in an attempt to dance.

Behind the stage it is just as muddy as in front. Paul Weller, foolishly dressed in a pair of white trousers, is gingerly tip-toeing around watched by the day's compere Alexei Sayle: "I don't know why you don't all go home," he mutters.

After an appearance by Australian rockers Midnight Oil, Sayle takes the stage to fill the gap before The Style Council. "I've got an announcement," he booms at the crowd as they stand in inches of muck. "Somebody has lost a contact lens out there." The crowd groans at the joke.

As the opening chords of "You're The Best Thing" strike up, thousands of muddy feet begin the laborious trek towards the main stage as Weller (who's now wisely changed his trousers) and Talbot romp enthusiastically through a selection of favourites – it's the *least* they can do for the wet crowd standing out in the drizzle.

"This one," announces Weller, "is called 'Long Hot Summer'."

Laugh? I almost cried.

William Shaw

"Well, it's dry up *here, mates!*" The Style Council cheer up the sodden masses.

Through slime and raging torrents flee the thousands! (*Anything* to escape the terrible jokes of Alexei Sayle).

"Ver wevver?" says Weller, "It's a Thatcherist ploy to undermine ver kids, innit?"

Alexei tells the one about Noah's mother-in-law and the flood. (Not v. funny in the circumstances . . .)

Back at base, a hardy couple do the time-honoured Hippie Festival Rain Dance.

Then came the problems of getting everyone home. Cars, buses, and vans just could not move. Breakdown trucks became victims of the mud, along with those they were trying to rescue. In the end, tractors were the only possible means of towing people off the site.

As the daunting task of clearing up began, Michael was proud of the way his staff and helpers had coped. "In the past my critics have said 'He was lucky with the weather, wait until he gets a mud-bath down there'. Well we have had the mud-bath and proved that we could still cope with the conditions." Let's hope he never has to again!

GLASTONBURY
CND FESTIVAL 1986
20-21-22 June. Worthy Farm. Pilton. Shepton Mallet. Somerset. BA4 4BY. Tel: Pilton (074989) 254/470 Telex No. 46404. TELADXG.
GLASTONBURY
CND FESTIVAL 1986
20-21-22 JUNE WORTHY FARM PILTON SHEPTON MALLET SOMERSET
Three-Day Festival Ticket
038387
£17.00
GLASTONBURY
CND FESTIVAL
20-21-22 June. Worthy Farm. Pilton. Somerset
ON STAGE
PASS PASS
Name
GLASTONBURY
CND FESTIVAL
20-21-22 June. Worthy Farm. Pilton. Somerset
BACK STAGE
PASS PASS
Name
1986

MIDSUMMER MADNESS

Pop man's swan song

THREAT TO END FESTIVAL

By John Turner

POP festival has farmer Mike Eavis has threatened to scrap CND's biggest fund-raising event.

Mr Eavis who owns Worthy Farm, Pilton, Shepton Mallet, the scene of this weekend's Glastonbury Festival said: "There are too many people and too many problems.

He said there [illegible] traffic chaos on roads [illegible] miles around.

Police towed [illegible] more than 100 [illegible] parked on verges a[illegible] narrow lanes su[illegible] ing the site.

No one reall[illegible] how many wer[illegible] site today; [illegible] ranged from [illegible] 100,000.

Mr Eavis [illegible]

MICHAEL EAVIS ... problems.

"I think there will be no festival in 1987. I might change my mind but I doubt it."

23,000 people arrived on Thursday night.

Cars towed away by the police were being taken to the Royal Bath and West Showground.

Superintendent David Coggan said his men had been working hard all night towing away nearly 150 cars.

People were still being arrested on drug offences he said.

Drug arrests totalled 116 by this morning an special courts were set up at Shepton Mallet.

Quantities of cannabis, LSD and amphetamines have been seized.

Dangerous drugs, in[illegible] [illegible]orphine, are [illegible]lating

By the end of the 1986 festival, Michael and Jean had made up their minds that they needed a rest. It had been the biggest festival of all, but the very success of the event nearly led to its demise. "There are too many people and too many problems. We're taking a break to recover" said Michael. They faced huge bills. The mountain of organisational and human problems had left them physically and emotionally exhausted. They were appalled at the amount of theft on the site — of course most of the punters had had a wonderful time, but they had not been the ones to turn up at the farmhouse having lost everything. It had all been too much.

As usual preparations had begun very early in the New Year. One of the first tasks is to choose the artwork, including the year's distinctive festival logo, which will appear on tickets, letter headings, T-shirts and publicity handouts. Several artists compete for the commission, a decision is reached, the printers do their work, then letters go out, advertising begins to appear and tickets are distributed to their points of sale.

By Easter, most of the crew have organised their rotas of helpers, market traders' licences have been issued and Michael already has a shrewd idea of the final Main Stage line up, except for inevitable last minute disappointments and surprises. Preparations then carry on right up to the festival, with every day bringing new decisions to be made and new problems to be overcome.

Stonehenge created the first and most enduring problem. The banning of the midsummer festival there led to large numbers of would-be attenders coming instead to Pilton. Despite some sympathy for the travellers who have come to be known as the Peace Convoy, the festival organisers knew only too well the damage that could be done if they arrived at Worthy Farm in large numbers two weeks before the event. Some did come and some caused problems, but to their great credit many realised Michael's impossible position and moved on after one or two nights rest, so as not to "foul things up for him and CND". In the months since then Michael and Jean have spent a great deal of time and effort trying to find a suitable site for the Stonehenge Festival, as near as possible to the stones.

By now it was June and the site crew had assembled. In three weeks they would transform a sleepy dairy farm into the busiest festival site in Europe, laying electricity and telephone cables, putting in water mains, excavating trenches for the lavatories and, all around the farm repairing this and repainting that.

On the weekend before the festival, a fleet of tractors cut the grass for silage making. Goose Hall the crew's canteen, swung into operation. One by one the marquees went up and the first traders began to arrive. The gates were set up and from that moment on you needed a ticket or a pass to get onto the site.

NO
ENTRY

By Thursday 19th June, the farm Office and the Communications, Welfare and Medical teams were all ready as the crowds began to drift in.

RADIOPHONES
41 DOCTOR
42 M. EAVIS
43 GATE+TRAFFIC
44 SITE MANAGER
45
STEANBOW
47 T HOLLINGSWORTH
AVALON 912
TELEPHONE SYSTEM
21 FARM OFFICE
FORD GATE
23 MAIN STAGE
24 THEATRE
25 TICKET CABIN
26 SITE KITCHEN
27 UPPER MARKET
28 LOWER MKT.
29 WELFARE
20 INFORMATION
31 MEDICAL
32 TRADER'S GATE
33 GATE+TRAFFIC
34 CHILDREN
35 COMMS
36 MAIN EXIT
37 COMMS
38 FOLK TENT
39 SECOND STAGE
30 CATTLE GRID
41 DOCTOR
42 M. EAVIS
43
44 SITE MANAGER
45 SECURITY
STEANBOW
47 T. HOLLINGSWORTH
48 GREEN FIELD
SECURITY
40 FIRST AID
51 BEER VILLAGE
52 COCKMILL GATE
EMERGENCY BARRIER KEY
FUEL STORE KEY
TONKA KEYS

FESTIVAL WELFA E

RESCUE CENTRE
LOST ANIMALS
IS THIS HUMANITY?
HEAVENS GATE
ANIMAL RESCUE
CENTRE

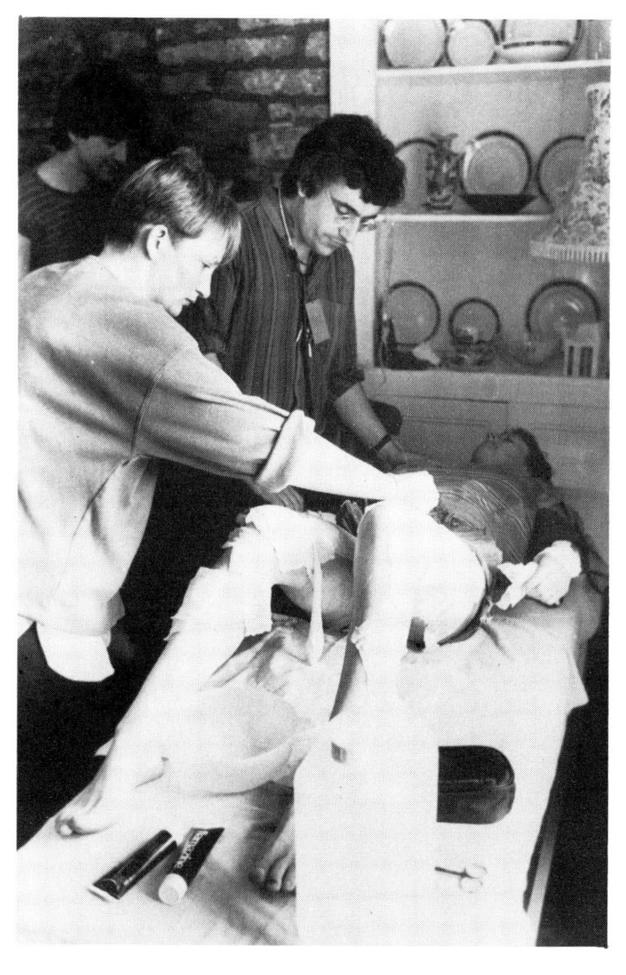

MEDICAL
CENTRE

AMBULANCE
AMBULANCE
RANGE ROVER

MEDICAL
CENTRE

Just how many people attend the Festival has always been a controversial point. Whose estimate is to be believed? How many tickets have been sold? How many got in without one? The local authority were convinced their attendance limits had been exceeded in previous years, but had been unable to prove it. This time the licence they granted was worded differently; there would be no limit set on numbers but sufficient facilities had to be provided for all the people who came. In order to establish more accurate attendance figures they hired a spotter plane to take aerial photographs of the crowd. However, according to one paper, it appears that every time the plane flew over 'thousands of people crawled into their tents' to reduce the apparent numbers. They tried counting the tents and doubling that figure, but the result — 36,000 — was rather unconvincing. The problem remained unresolved.

A second festival entrance had to be provided to reduce the amount of traffic congestion in Pilton village. This was established through a neighbouring farm to the west of the site, the intention being to open it on Thursday and Friday when most people were expected to arrive. However, it proved impossible to admit traffic quickly enough through this new gate, causing an enormous tail-back on the Glastonbury road. Meanwhile the Main Entrance continued to cope with the majority of arrivals. Here too, there were long queues and local people were inconvenienced considerably for a time, as the population of the little village expanded to that of a sizeable town.

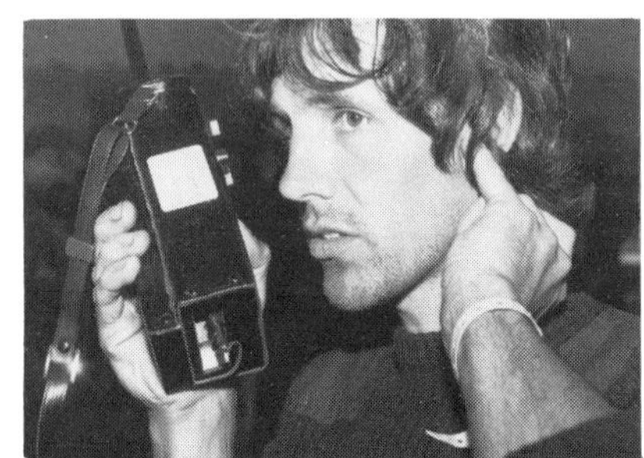

Once on site, the long waits in traffic queues could soon be forgotten. There were two market areas to explore — the original at the top of the hill adjacent to the farm buildings, and the newer one further down the site which had been established in '85 and now considerably enlarged. In either you could lose yourself in the crowds, jostling through the maze of stalls, tents, vans and caravans, offering food and drink, clothes and crafts, games and toys, records and tapes, blankets and sleeping bags. Double decker buses stood colourfully above the crowds — the red of the Labour Party, the rainbow of Greenpeace, and the distinctive livery of the Pennine Pizza Express.

A survey conducted amongst some of the traders revealed that the majority came from the West, Wales and London, mostly to make money, but many giving 'CND' and 'to have fun' as their reasons for being there. Most thought Glastonbury better than other festivals, and nearly all of them wanted to come back, despite the problems of access and refuse disposal a good number seemed to have experienced.

BEAU NOSH
Motörhead

BREAKFAST

OUR CIDER IS STRONG
OUR CIDER IS ECOLOGICAL
OUR CIDER WINS PRIZES

EX-SERVICES
C.N.D.
HAPPY FESTIVAL
Delicious Home made cakes

ZAC
JANEEN

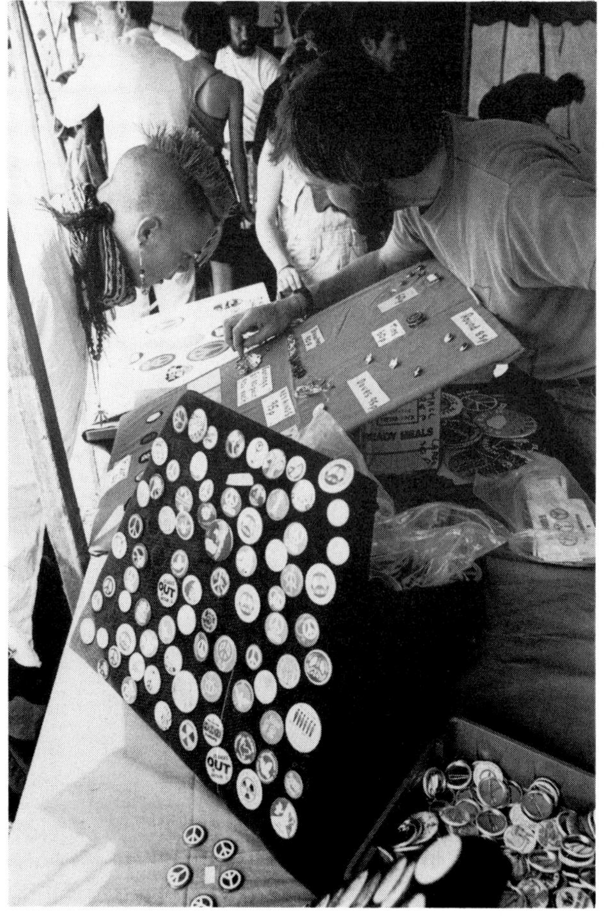

FLUSH LOOS

TOILETS
FIRE ALAR
USE ONLY IN EMERGE
FIRE BUC
IF YOU DON'T WANT TO SPEND 4 DAYS IN HERE WITH DIARRHOEA
WASH YOUR HANDS AFTER PLEASE
WASH YOUR HANDS PLEASE

FIRE ALARM
IN EMERGENCY

WATER
FIRE ALARM
USE ONLY IN EMERGENCIES
FIRE BUCKETS

Payphones
Payphones

Theatre was to be found in a new location, a flat spacious field with two marquees and an open air stage, not to mention two cafes. Here too, the Glastonbury Global newspaper had its base.

Prominent attractions amongst the three hundred or so performers gathered by Arabella Churchill and her colleagues were Denise Black and the Kray Sisters, Joolz, The Greatest Show on Legs, Sensible Footwear, Akimbo, and Haggis and Charlie in the marquees, with acts like Circus Dropalot, Balls-up Jugglers, Desperate Men and the Flying Bin-Lids keeping up non-stop entertainment outside.

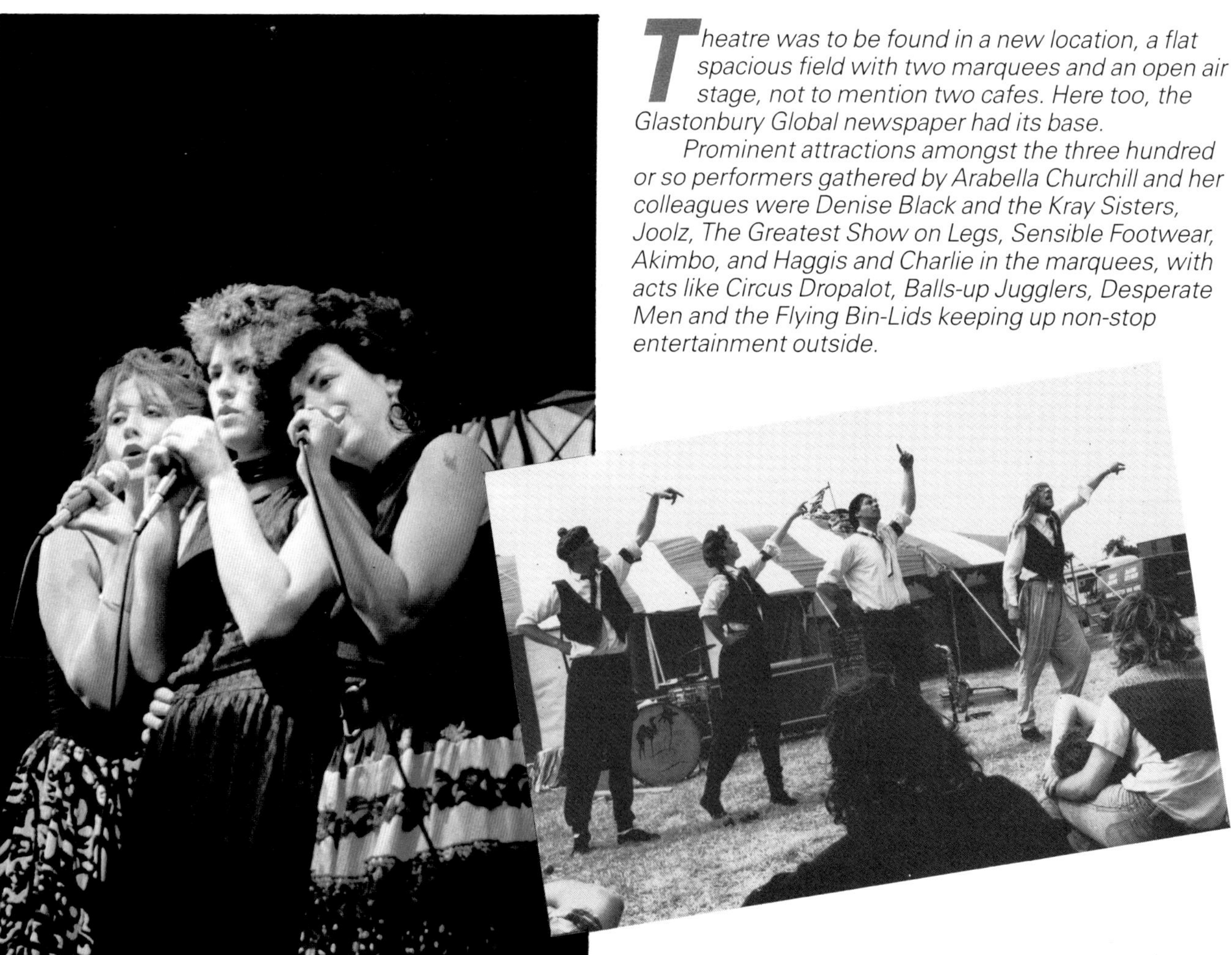

BOYCOTT
NOT

Like Theatre, the Children's Area had a new home. As the festival had grown, its old position just off the main thoroughfare to the Arena had become unsuitable, so a much more peaceful situation was found next to the Acoustic and Classical Stages.

A number of permanent structures, installed over the years, needed to be carefully dismantled and rebuilt on the new sloping site. Mike Orchard and Stephanie Lalond, who spent many hours poring over the plans; and the builders, David, Charlie and Paul, did a fine job. The new siting in its haven of tranquillity was greatly appreciated by many families.

HIGH

SAUNA

FABULOUS BICYCLE POWERED

Another place to go when the bustle and noise got too much was the Green Field, with its distinctive totem and teepee circle, beautiful gardens created by Kate Stanley, thought-provoking displays of alternative technology, and craft demonstrations using natural materials, as well as live entertainment and debate. Here you could find solace, and take advantage of the breath-taking view over the whole site before venturing back to the markets, marquees and music.

660 BCJ
9542 PT

Classical Stage
1.30 Alan Schiller
3.30 Fulleylove Trio
6.00 Richard Stagg
the Hisako Maeda
7.00 Subculture
9.30 Electric Chamber
Ensemble
Unfortunately John
Williams is unable to
play due to flu.

Music of every kind abounded. Never far away at any hour of the day or night was the inevitable reggae from a thousand ghetto-blasters.

The perfect counterpoint to this insistent beat was provided in the elegant blue Classical marquee, away in a quiet corner of the site. Here in this restful setting audiences were delighted by members of the musicians own anti-nuclear organisation, Musicians Against Nuclear Arms.

John Williams, who had been largely responsible for arranging this part of the festival, was prevented from appearing by illness, but Alan Schiller, Gerald Garcia, Kaleidoscope, Sub-Culture and the rest combined to make up for the disappointment caused by his absence. Once drawn into this oasis, most people found themselves held in its magic, reluctant to break the spell.

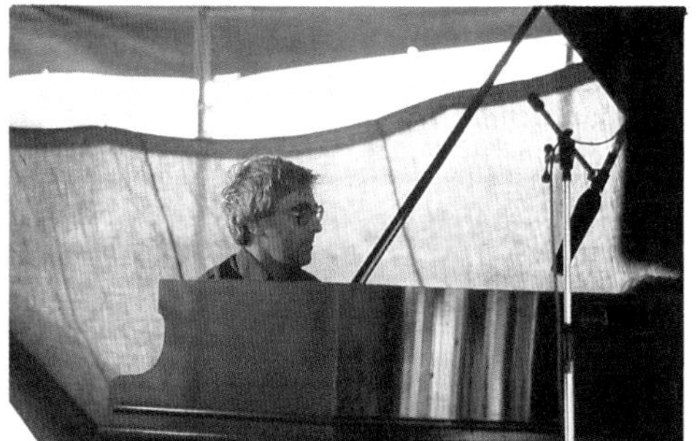

Many performers who could have commanded a place on the Pyramid appeared instead on the Acoustic Stage, their talents being considered better suited to its more intimate environment. What a tribute to the depth of talent attracted to the festival that one of its subsidiary stages could boast artists of the quality of Maria Muldour, The Mint Juleps, Rumillajta from South America, Billy Bragg and Loudon Wainwright III. Loudon, in fact, did play a further set on the Main Stage. As for Billy Bragg, he popped up on both the Acoustic and Second Stages — he just wanted to be there.

On Stage Two, traditionally a stepping-stone to greater things, Fuzzbox, Half Man Half Biscuit, Frank Chickens, Pauline Black and the Supernaturals and the Mighty Lemon Drops all appeared.

STUDIO 34
BRISTOL ENGLAND

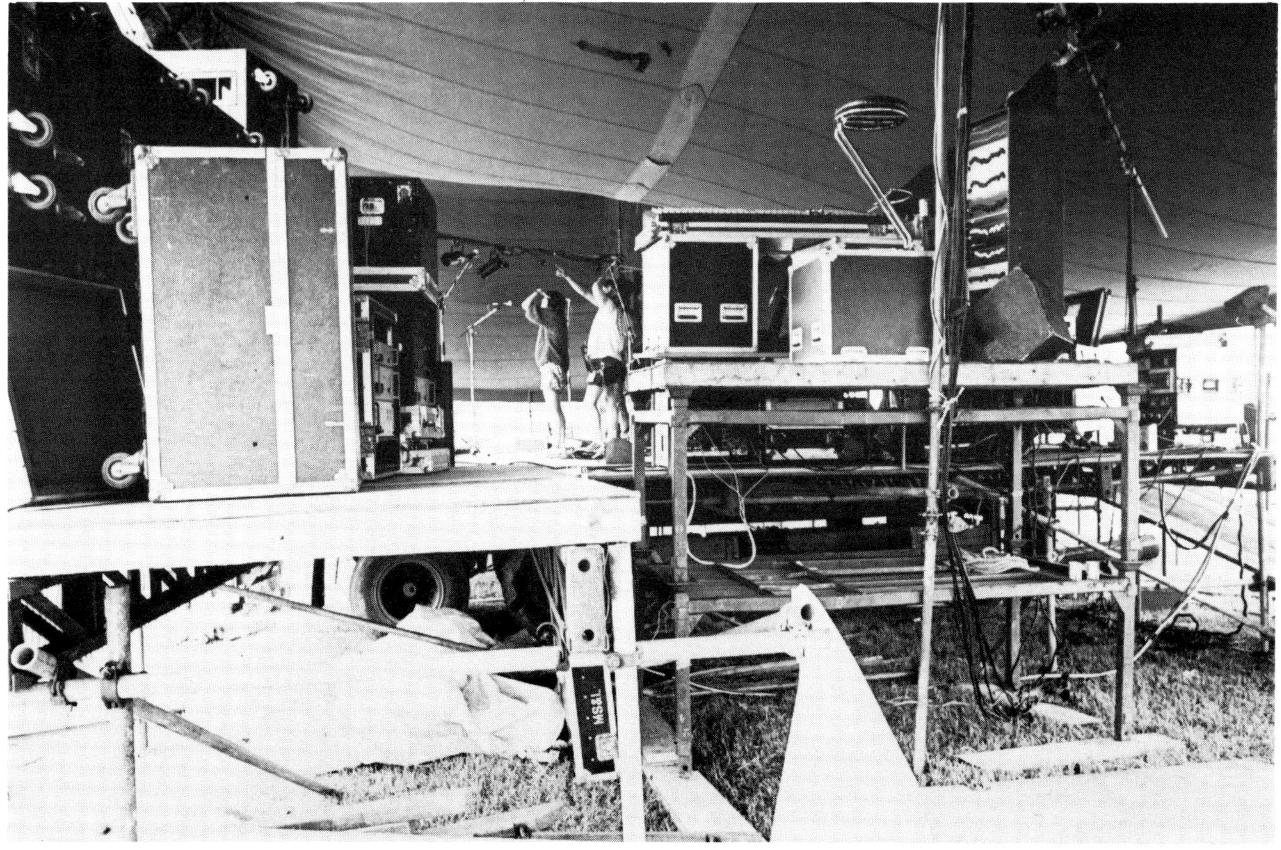

Meanwhile, elsewhere on site . . .

One of the last areas of the site to come together is the main Pyramid Stage. Only a few days before the first band was due to play, the stage was cleared of all the litter drums, chairs, water barrels and so on stored there from the previous year. The mixing tower was erected, up went the lighting gantries and the vast speaker stacks were put in place at either side of the stage. In the midst of all this a BBC film crew was at work with Michael Wood, wearer of the tightest jeans in television history, recording part of his "Domesday" series.

Some changes were made to overcome problems encountered in previous years. For a few, the heady atmosphere, the close proximity of the bands and the disinhibiting effects of alcohol can prove a little too much. The temptation to climb up the front of the Pyramid onto the stage, or to indulge in a little mud-throwing becomes irresistible. Firstly, a sturdy crash barrier was put up in front of the Pyramid, the area within it under the watchful eye of a special security team. This not only helped to protect the artists on stage, but also improved the lot of those at the front of the crowd who obtained a far better view of the performance.

The other change was the removal of the beer tent from the Arena. Anyone who really wanted a drink would have to walk all the way up to the Market Area to get one, with the prospect of sobering up at least a little on the way.

However successful the festival may be, it would be nothing without the crowds who come back year after year.

As Waterboy Mike Scott put it "It's the people's festival. It's good and it's real and people come."

And come they do from all over the world. But how far you've travelled and how long it took you to get there is immaterial — being there is what matters.

DISCHARGE

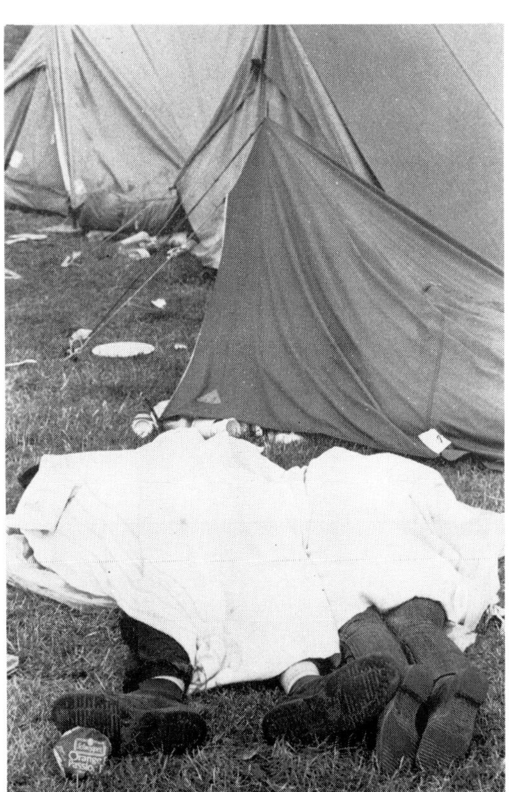

There was always a lot of activity in the backstage compound. Huge pantechnicons deliver the bands' equipment while the performers themselves are ferried in and out in large luxury coaches. In the background the mighty generators rumble.

And so many people — the bands and all their travelling entourages, the compères, the speakers, the stage crews, the sound and lighting engineers, the security staff, the journalists and photographers, the medical personnel, the catering staff, the groupies, the roadies and countless guests.

But in all this hubbub of activity behind the scenes, the backstage crew seemed relaxed and confident — everyone knew what had to be done and got on with it.

Truck Rental

Howard Hughes and the Western Approaches kicked off on Friday afternoon, followed by Irish band That Petrol Emotion. They have a lot to say about the situation in Ireland through their rough, strained pop noise, both of colossal hope and of a deep sense of loss. "That petrol emotion" is a term used in Northern Ireland to describe a feeling that is almost inexpressible, a frustration you feel when you are living there — anger and despair about the whole thing. Their sound is drawn from a wide range of influences but ends up sounding like no-one but themselves. They played a moving set.

Later on CND Chairman Paul Johns, making his first visit to Glastonbury, addressed the crowd from the Pyramid Stage. Afterwards in the backstage cafe, he spoke warmly of the festival, and in particular of the way it had helped create a closer relationship between the Campaign and the music business which had been very beneficial to the movement. He was also very appreciative of the huge financial support given to CND by the festival and hoped very much that Michael would feel able to continue with it in future years.

Next to appear was one of the best received Main Stage acts of the whole weekend — The Waterboys. Leader Mike Scott has been described by some as one of the most gifted people in the business. His music is about honour, and magic, and emotions. It's about strength, it's about love. Their set included "Meet me at the Station", "The Wayward Wind", "Fisherman's Blues", and several numbers from their "This is the Sea" album. Afterwards backstage, Mike and saxophonist Anthony Thistlethwaite recalled that for a long time they had been thinking about Glastonbury and about coming here. They felt the '80s to be a time of public awakening — "Things like Live Aid caused more people to be aware of what is going on in the world" said Mike, and the CND movement was getting people thinking, especially now with the US missiles here in our country, 'Cruise is an awful kick in the teeth' ".

This was the Waterboys' second visit to Glastonbury. They admitted to having been "terrified" before going on stage back in '84. But this time with a couple more years' experience behind them and the special feeling they said they sensed coming over from the crowd, there were no such fears.

The Pogues came back this year and their rollicking inebriated set enthralled their assembled fans "whose loyalty is awesome". Between swigs of beer they blasted out numbers from their recently released "Poguetry in Motion" album. The crowd were stunned with a mixture of emotions. It all went down very well, both the booze and the music.

In complete contrast, next to appear on the Main Stage was the lady who has been acclaimed as the best new soul voice in Britain for years, Ruby Turner. She held everyone's attention with her polished performance and sensitive style. Very easy, very pleasurable.

The Psychedelic Furs topped the bill on Friday evening, and their performance was magnificent. It was not only the visual effects which astounded the fans, but the slick delivery of each number and the vivacious style of lead singer Richard Butler got the vibes reaching out across the valley. The crowds were sent wild by this truly memorable performance.

Saturday's line-up was just as impressive. Local hero Rodney Allen was first to appear, and for someone little known outside the area, attracted a considerable amount of approval from the crowd. His style, not unlike Billy Bragg's, is punchy and to the point, covering teenage emotions and the pitfalls they encounter on the road to adulthood. He believes in himself, and by the end of his act had the crowd believing too.

Next on stage were the Grasshoppers, with lead singer Buddy Curtess. The nine members of this soul/rock and roll band cover mostly the music of the 50s and early 60s, mixing oldies with originals in a very lively and exciting style. Their's was a colourful and entertaining set.

Loudon Wainwright III appeared, clad in shorts and baseball cap, and had a bemused crowd singing along as he climaxed his brief performance with "Dead Skunk in the Middle of the Road".

Next came John Martyn who has been playing open air festivals for as long as anyone can remember. After a relaxed start he built up the tempo and drove his excellent band to a storming finish.

Top reggae band Black Uhuru — back at Glastonbury for the third time — were next on. Ducky Simpson, Junior Reid and the beautiful Puma Jones didn't disappoint their waiting fans. On this occasion they were joined by two of the legendary Wailers, formally of course with the late Bob Marley.

At 9 pm came one of the big new bands of the 80s — Lloyd Cole and the Commotions. They included a selection from their recent "Easy Pieces" album. Afterwards in the backstage bar Lloyd Cole admitted that he wasn't really a festival person, but Glastonbury and everything it stood for was different. He thought everyone should be on the side of CND, and that the banning and dismantling of nuclear weapons was essential for world peace.

GLASTONBURY
CND FESTIVAL
20·21·22 June. Worthy Farm Pilton Somerset
ON STAGE
PASS PASS
Name
1986

YAMAHA

UNCLE BUD'S
CATFISH
FRANKLIN, TENNESSEE

By the end of this set the heavens had opened and an incredible display of thunder and lightning, which momentarily lit up the whole of the site, erupted over Worthy Farm. It was not long before the whole site was a sea of shallow mud. The ground had been hard baked and well trodden, and this unexpected torrent was too much for the soil to soak up; it ran away in tiny rivers down the hillsides.

The atmosphere was already electric by the time the last band of the evening came onto the stage. And soon it was even more highly charged as The Cure appeared in a swirling cloud of sulphurous smoke. Who better to bring the evening's events to a spectacular close.

The "fourth best band in Hull" stepped on to the stage at 12 noon on Sunday. The Housemartins are widely known for putting over political points in their lyrics, and Glastonbury was the ideal place to let them be heard; a unique band whose following grows with every live performance and each new release. The reception they got showed this to be true.

Next to appear was Christy Moore, no stranger to Glastonbury and another performer who expresses his strong political convictions in his music. As well as the troubles in his native Ireland, the songs in his moody and haunting set dealt with a whole range of other issues, including nuclear weapons.

Robert Cray broke off from his British Tour to make an appearance at Glastonbury. His style recalls the heyday of blues and soul in the '60s, revamped to bring each number right up to date. His expressive guitar and versatile vocal delivery, backed up by his superb band combined to make this an outstanding and memorable performance.

Simply Red is another band with strong anti-nuclear views. Hailed as one of Britain's finest white soul singers, Mick Hucknall has undoubtedly been greatly influenced by the music of the '60s. He led the band through an emotional set, letting his audience bask in the comfortable warmth of his more soulful numbers, and then jerking them harshly back to reality with his stark political lyrics. As he sang "Holding Back the Years", and "Money's Too Tight" a few people here and there were dancing, and the Arena was filled with a moving forest of outstretched arms swaying above the heads of the crowd.

7pm — the evening sun shining down the valley, the Pyramid glistening in the golden light, and the fields swathed in the rich green of midsummer. People gathered in the Arena, and soon they stood shoulder to shoulder, eyes raised in expectation, looking towards the stage. A dozen security men filed into the no-go area between the crash barrier and the stage. As his last record finished, Andy Kershaw on his platform high above the stage announced the next band. Madness.

Bounding into view lead singer Suggs cheerily greeted the crowd "allo. What a luverly day". Their happy, lively set included such favourites as "Take it or leave it", "Baggy Trousers", "House of Fun", "My Girl" and "It must be Love", and ended with "Our House". Out came the giant balloons.

With their set over Suggs made for the backstage café to suffer along with the rest of the little crowd packed around the TV as Argentina knocked England out of the World Cup.

For the next band too, Glastonbury was not just another gig, but an opportunity to identify publicly with the anti-nuclear cause. Level 42 are a top funk/blues band featuring the extraordinary bass playing of Mark King, whose hands are reputed to be insured for £1m. Since their formation in 1980, their remarkable success has taken the pop world by storm. They launched into a varied selection of their songs drawn from their five albums and included "The Sun Goes Down", "Chinese Way", and "Lessons in Love". Although Mark is recognised as leader of the band, each of its members is an outstandingly gifted musician, and it is the combination of their remarkable talents which produces the band's very individual sound.

Gil Scott-Heron has for many years used his music to express his feelings on a wide range of political issues. It all began with the struggle for civil rights back home in America. Then with the advent of the Thatcher/Reagan partnership, his anti-nuclear message "Shut Um Down" gained wide acclaim, as did his tribute to the President — "ReRon".

As Gil's final number brought the evening to a close, the lasers were there to round off the whole weekend with a thrillingly spectacular display. Reluctantly, the crowd turned away from the Pyramid for the last time, and as the Arena slowly emptied, the forgotten sounds of the markets and campsites gradually re-emerged — the dull throb of generators, the subdued rhythms of taped music, and the comfortable hum of late night conversation.

THE AFTERMATH

In the early hours of Monday morning the big clean up began. Dust carts trundled onto the site, devouring refuse filled bags as they went. The skips scattered around the site, now loaded to the brim with festival debris, were hoisted up and driven away.

Meanwhile the motley army of litter pickers, bent low over their unenvied task, swept gradually across the fields removing all traces of the weekend's accumulated rubbish.

For those among them who had heartfelt feelings about the ecology of the place, it was their way of showing how they cared for the land, and saying thank you.

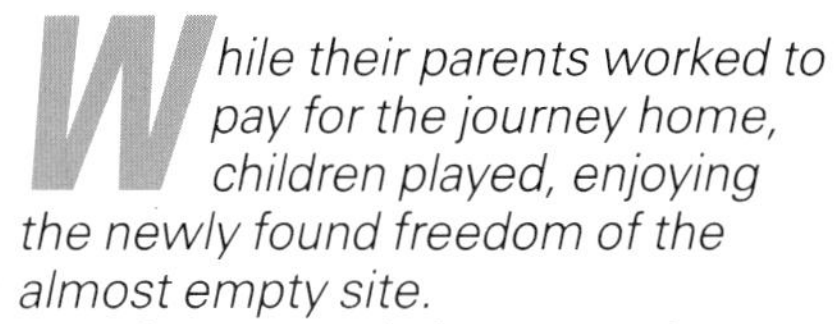

While their parents worked to pay for the journey home, children played, enjoying the newly found freedom of the almost empty site.

Some people just stayed on because they couldn't bear to leave this magical place — a place which had cast its spell over all those who had come. A three-day-long dream from which we were reluctant to awaken.

But would it all happen again next year? There had been so much that had been worthwhile, yet the exhausted crew wondered if it had all grown too big and unmanageable. They had spent so much time sorting out problems caused by people being selfish, thoughtless or dishonest. There was even talk of not having a festival in 1987, but deep down, as they too drifted homewards for a bath and a long sleep, they knew that magic would bring them back next year to do it all again.

As the last stragglers left the farm, the cows reclaimed the land.

Peter Ball (Canning/Emery)

Penny Mellor (Hammond/Cooper)

Arabella Churchill (Marcus Cole)

Robert Ingle and Paul Scott (Donald Scaife)

Pat Wilson and Dan Plesch (Appleton/Smith)

Andrew Kerr (Jeremy Hooper)

Mark and Helen Cann (Jeremy Hooper)

Chris Howes (Paul Walters)

Glen Smith (Jeremy Hooper)

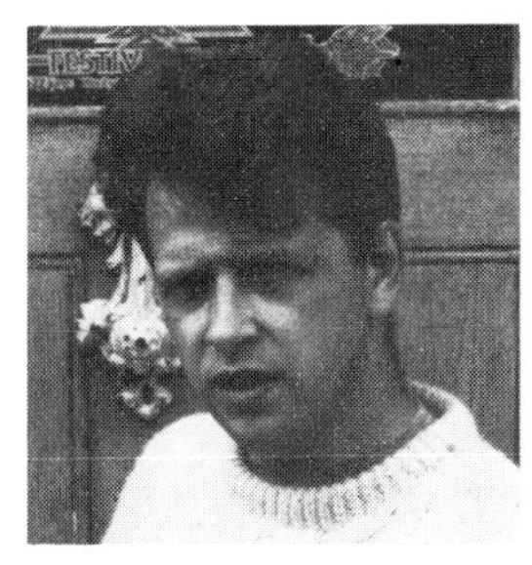

Tony Hollingsworth (Jeremy Hooper)

Thomas Crimble, Nutkin, Debbie and Justine (Jeremy Hooper)

Henri and Kevin (Tim Malyon)

Mike Denner (Marcus Cole)

Pilton Palais/Cinema.

John Allen

Johnny Allen is a member of the site crew who works on the farm all year. He has been responsible for much of the beautiful stonework around the farm.

Mike Orchard (Canning/Emery)

Mandy Scholefield (Appleton/Smith)

Nick Scholefield (Appleton/Smith)

David Ansonia (Marcus Cole)

Charlie Wrighton (Tim Malyon)

Charlie Wrighton has been a member of the team for many years. He is the one who produces 3 meals-a-day for some 250 members of the Site Crew, not only during the Festival but for several weeks before and after the event.

Richard Lawson (Kevin Redpath)

Sarah Davis (Canning/Emery)

Stephanie Leland (Francine Stainthorp)

Kim McGavin

Kim McGavin and Ann Waterhouse are responsible for the running of the Green Field on behalf of the Green Collective.

Photo credits:
t:top, b: botton, c: centre, l: left, r: right

Jeremy Hooper:
6; 10; 67b; 68t; 70cl, cr; 72b; 73bl; 74t, cl; 75cr, br; 100c, b; 103br; 104tl, br; 105t, cr, bl; 107t; 108tr; 110cr, br; 113c; 118tr, br; 123tl, tr, br; 124t, bl; 125b; 127tl, cl; 131t, cr; 132t; 134cl; 135cl, tr.

Donald Scaife:
72t; 73t, 74b; 75bl; 78bl; 79bl; 80b; 83bl; 84b; 94bl; 95; 96bl, br; 102c, 109cr, br; 120c; 128bl, br; 129tr, c, b; 134t, cr; 135t, bl.

Jan Hammond and Neil Cooper *(Framework):*
67c; 69b; 77bl, br; 78cl, br; 79br; 81tl, cl; 82tr, br; 83tl, tr, cl; 84tl; 85br; 87t; 89bl; 91b; 92t; 93tl, b; 94c; 98tr; 99tl, tr; 106tr; 108tl, bl, br; 109bl; 113b; 118cl; 120br; 135br.

Tim Malyon *(Framework):*
Front and Back Cover. 16br; 32; 33; 41; 44tl; tr, cr, bl; 45tr, b; 46t, c; 47cl; 128t; 133tr, b; 134b.

Bob Canning and Tony Emery:
10tl; 13; 68br; 69t; 70tl, tr; 71cl, cr; 73c, br; 76br; 79t; 80c; 81tr, cr; 82tl; 83br; 84tr; 86tr, b; 88; 89br; 90tl, tr, cr, bl, br; 94t, br; 96cr, 97tl; 98tl; 99cl; 101cr; 104tr; 106/7; 108tr; 109cr; 110tr, cl, bl; 111; 112; 113tr, tl; 114tl, tr; 115b; 118tl; 119; 120t, bl; 123bl; 126; 127br; 136b; 137; 144.

Paul Walters *(South-West News):*
75tl; 110tl.

Mendip D.C.:
27tr; 28cl; 29b; 45cl.

Every effort has been made to credit all photographs accurately. We apologise for any errors or omissions.

Kevin Redpath:
4; 50; 52bl; 56; 57b; 60tl, c, b; 61br; 62c; 63; 64tl; 65; 77t; 78t; 80tl, tr; 85t; 87c; 97b; 109t; 115tr; 116b; 133tl.

Andy Liguz:
114b; 115tl; 117b; 118cr; 121; 122tr, c, b; 127bl; 132b.

Cathy Appleton and Erica Smith *(Indent)*:
12; 68bl; 70br; 71bl; 72c; 76t; 85bl; 87b; 89cl; 90cl; 92c, b; 93tr; 97tr; 99b.

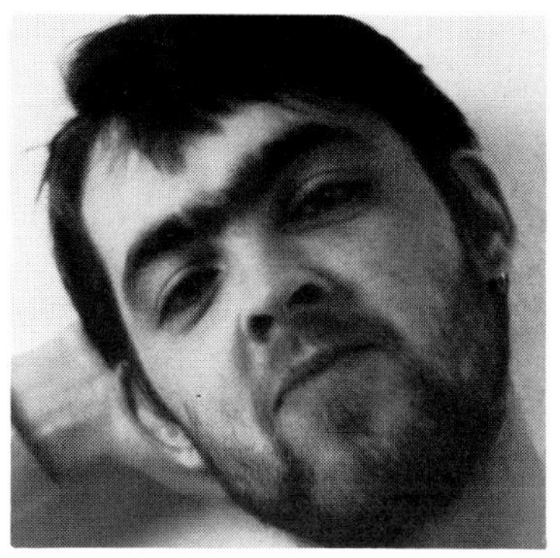

Marcus Cole:
70bl; 71t, br; 74cr; 76bl; 81b; 82bl; 86tl; 93cr; 96t, cl; 98b; 100t; 101t, cl, b; 102t, b; 103t, bl; 104c; 115c; 116t, c; 117t, c; 124br; 125t; 129tl; 131cl, b; 132c; 136tl.

Ron Reid:
13cl, cr; 14br, tr, tl; 15t; 16t, cr; 18tl, b; 19b, cl, cr; 20br; 21; 22l, cr, br; 31.

Brian Walker:
10; 11; 13; 14bl; 15b; 16cl, bl; 17; 18tr; 19tr; 20tl, tr, cr, bl; 22tr; 26br; 27tl; 28tr, bl, br; 29t, cl, cr; 34; 35; 38c, b; 39br; 40; 44br; 45t; 47tl, bl; 49; 51; 52br; 53; 54; 57tl, tr; 60tr; 61t, c, bl, bfl; 62tl, tr, bl, br; 64tr; 79cl; 89t; 91t; 105br; 106tl; 127tr; 130.

Born in London, Anne is a State Registered Nurse and has lived in the West Country for 20 years, settling in nearby Shepton Mallet in 1978.

She is married to a local doctor and has two children, Catherine and Daniel. Together with her husband Chris, she has been involved in the organisation of medical services at the Festival for the past seven years.

Her interest in popular music began with the Stones and Beatles in the mid-sixties, when she worked as a secretary and fashion model in the West End of London.

She is a member of CND, Greenpeace and the Medical Campaign Against Nuclear Weapons.

Lynne comes from Southampton and spent her student years in Salford, Newcastle-upon-Tyne, Paris and the south of Spain before moving to Somerset in 1977.

She lives in Shepton Mallet with her husband Colin and sons Christopher and Robert, teaching part-time at the local sixth-form college.

For Lynne, a CND member and long-standing lover of rock and roll, the Festival has a magical appeal.

Anne Howes   Lynne Elstob